THE SOUTHWESTERN MEDICAL DISTRICT

Prehistory to the Future of Medicine

Evelyn Montgomery, PhD
with special contributions
by Robert Prejean

TEXAS TREES FOUNDATION

Published by Texas Trees Foundation

Printed and distributed
by Ingram Spark, a division of Ingram.

FIRST EDITION
ISBN: 979-8-3302142-7-3

Library of Congress Control Number: 2024942026

INTRODUCTION

Robert Prejean

In early December 2014, Janette Monear, then Executive Director of the Texas Trees Foundation, and her associate Matt Grubisich, Operations Director and Urban Forester, met with Robert Prejean, Manager of the Southwestern Medical District, to launch a proposal to landscape a portion of Harry Hines Boulevard—then a one-mile stretch of road to be called the "Medical Mile Transformational Greening Plan." The proposal would be led by Texas Trees Foundation but be done in partnership with the Southwestern Medical District. As they discussed the area and its growth along Harry Hines Boulevard, there was a shared interest in the history in and around the Medical District and a realization that little had been documented about this area as opposed to the histories of other Dallas communities. Through time and further iterations, the one-mile study became two, along with a broader scope; and, as the reader can imagine, a seed was planted.

This is a book that focuses on those areas northwest of today's downtown Dallas but generally within Loop 12. It begins by walking the reader back to a time when this region was a virgin landscape. Each page describes the land, creatures, people, and the many events that followed, providing an appreciation for what we know today about this area. Some will see this only as a history book, but its true value is how these events through time are attached to a setting that allows a fuller connection to place.

FOREWORD

Janette Monear

Winston Churchill once said, "The farther backward you look, the further forward you are likely to see," but it is hard to imagine that we would have entertained the vision of what exists in the Southwestern Medical District in the City of Dallas today. Three world-renowned hospitals—Parkland Health & Hospital System, Children's Health, and UT Southwestern Medical Center, all with additional services and businesses within the area—provide innovative and cutting-edge research and healthcare to more than three million patients per year with no less than 42,000 dedicated health care employees. A place of hope and healing, the Southwestern Medical District (SWMD) is the second largest employment center in the City of Dallas, serving world class care.

In the chapters that follow, we embark on a captivating journey through the history of Dallas' Medical District, exploring the intricate tapestry of its early life, settlement, urbanization, and healthcare evolution. From the harmonious coexistence of Native American tribes with the land, to the rise of healthcare institutions that have become cornerstones of the Medical District, leaders like Poncho Medrano, Karl Hoblitzelle, and Dr. Edward Cary were part of the evolving relationship between the past and the present. These historical insights from people and the land can inspire contemporary landscape design. This insight emphasizes the potential for innovation, mimicking the possibilities for the Southwestern Medical District Streetscape and Park transformation, ultimately creating a deeper connection to an area's history, its rich environment, and to oneself. These chapters thus unveil the layers of stories that have shaped this area, and in parallel, the city's past.

The Texas Trees Foundation has begun rewriting the story by leading a visionary, therapeutic landscape redesign to transform the antiquated Harry Hines corridor in the Southwestern Medical District into a vibrant, connected, and safe multi-model linear parkway with a eight-acre park at the intersection of Harry Hines Boulevard and Inwood Road. Through the lens of history and a robust equitable engagement process, the holistic restructuring will focus on evidence-based design to create a medical district focused on healthy systems, healthy people, and healthy environments.

For the Texas Trees Foundation, it is imperative to incorporate our changing relationship to the past into the landscape design. This history should serve as a vehicle for innovative design interventions that create imaginative places and evoke history in the present with new layers of meaning, and, through the creation of "new sacred places," enable different interpretations and narratives that emphasize the interconnections between history, place, identity, and community. Like the aspirations for the Streetscape and Park Project, the Foundation hopes this book will connect readers to the history of the landscape and help welcome ideas of what the district's future can be.

Committed to preserving the history of the region, the Foundation commissioned the book to be authored by Dr. Evelyn Montgomery and Robert Prejean. Dr. Montgomery is a Dallas historian and Director of the Old Red Museum of Dallas County History and Culture. Mr. Prejean is the manager of the Southwestern Medical District, and a passionate local historian with a background in urban planning.

Preface

"When I started researching the history of the Southwestern Medical District, I knew little about it and feared there might be little to discover. I was wrong! Though sometimes overlooked in Dallas history, the Medical District had Caddo tribes, pioneers, cattle, illegal gambling, medical, propeller planes overhead, funky roadside architecture, businesses like the Better Monkey Grip Company, and the home of Sam Tasby, the man who challenged Dallas to desegregate its schools and give his children an equal education. The book has five chapters before we even get to the amazing origin stories and world-changing accomplishments of the medical institutions!"

— Evelyn Montgomery, PhD

TABLE OF CONTENTS

Cover Description: Early bird's eye image of Dallas by Herman Brosius in 1872 is overlaid with a photo taken in 1947 at the site of the future Southwestern Medical District, whose boundaries today cover more than 1000 acres.

THE SOUTHWESTERN MEDICAL DISTRICT

Prehistory to the Future of Medicine

Evelyn Montgomery, PhD
with special contributions
by Robert Prejean

Chapter 1
EARLY LIFE ON THE LAND

The lands of the Medical District teemed with life long before Texian and American settlers arrived. Native Americans and the plants and animals they needed enjoyed life along the most important inhabitant of the area, the Elm Fork of the Trinity River. The river's water was the major attraction for everyone.

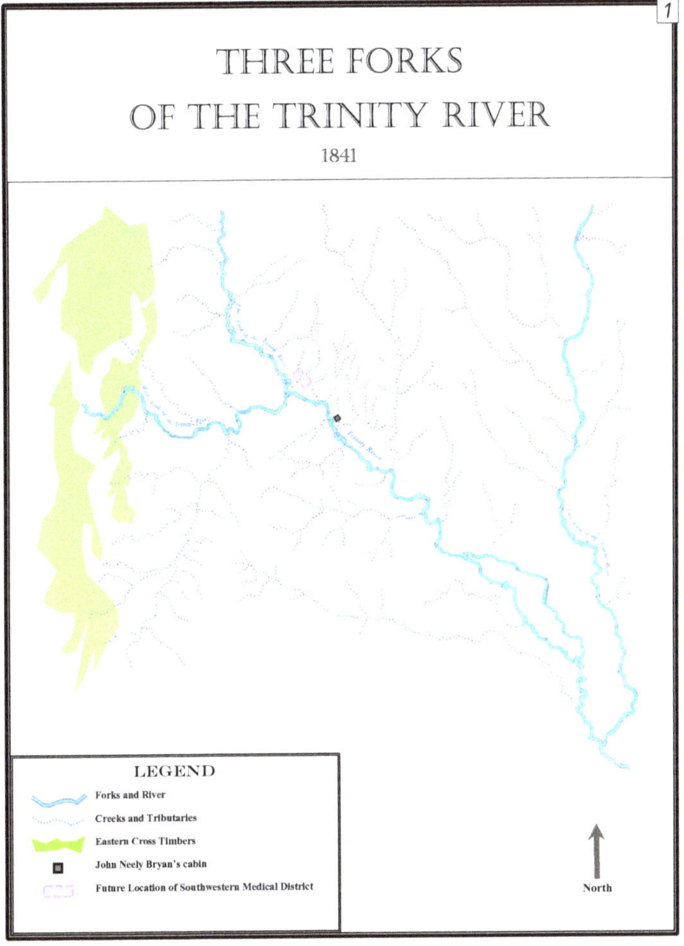

Figure 1: The Elm and West Forks, along with the East Fork, form the Three Forks that drew settlement to Dallas. Courtesy of Robert Prejean.

The broad river floodplain offered a moist environment with rich soil. It supported at least eighteen species of trees along its banks. Most were elm, hackberry, Spanish oak, or pecan, with the post oak well represented. The Bois d'Arc tree is also a native. It does not produce the long trunks useful for log cabins or milled lumber, but pioneers find a way to use every available resource. The twisting and intertwining nature of its branches could create a living fence when pioneers planted rows along their fields. Trunks planted in a line could support wire fencing. The tree's generous lifespan kept these on the urban landscape long after the agricultural period ended. Later uses included foundation supports for houses and blocks for road surfacing, both taking advantage of the species' rot resistance. Otherwise known as the "Osage Orange," the potential uses for its strong, durable wood were identified early in the regional settlement.[1] In 1905, the Bryan Lumber Company on Swiss Avenue advertised "wagon felloes and insulator Pins" of that sturdy wood.[2]

A much denser forest could be found further west—the Cross Timbers. This is a range of forest that runs north and south through northern Texas, Oklahoma, and Kansas. It forms a fork in Texas, with the eastern Cross Timbers descending between Fort Worth and Dallas. The Eastern Cross Timbers does not touch the Medical District, but for people moving west or northwest from Dallas County, the land that would one day be the Medical District was the last open land

Figure 2: Bois d'Arc trees are not common sights in Dallas today, but a few are maintained in city parks. Their unusual branch formations attract playful children and people interested in a unique photographic setting. This one is in Tietze Park on Skillman Street. Photo by Jim Rain, 2016, available through Wikimedia Commons courtesy of Jim Rain, available at [[File:TietzeBoisDArc2.jpg|TietzeBoisDArc2]].

before forest. Groves of Post Oaks, Pin Oaks, and Cedar trees did extend beyond the forest edge into the Medical District and down to the Cedars neighborhood just south of downtown.

---

1 Brady, William M. *Glimpses of Texas: its Divisions, Resources, Development and Prospects* (Houston: A. C. Gray & Company, Printers, 1871) p. 21.
2 All Saints Church, Ladies' Guild, *Hints to Housekeepers* (Dallas: All Saints Church, 1905), p. 9.

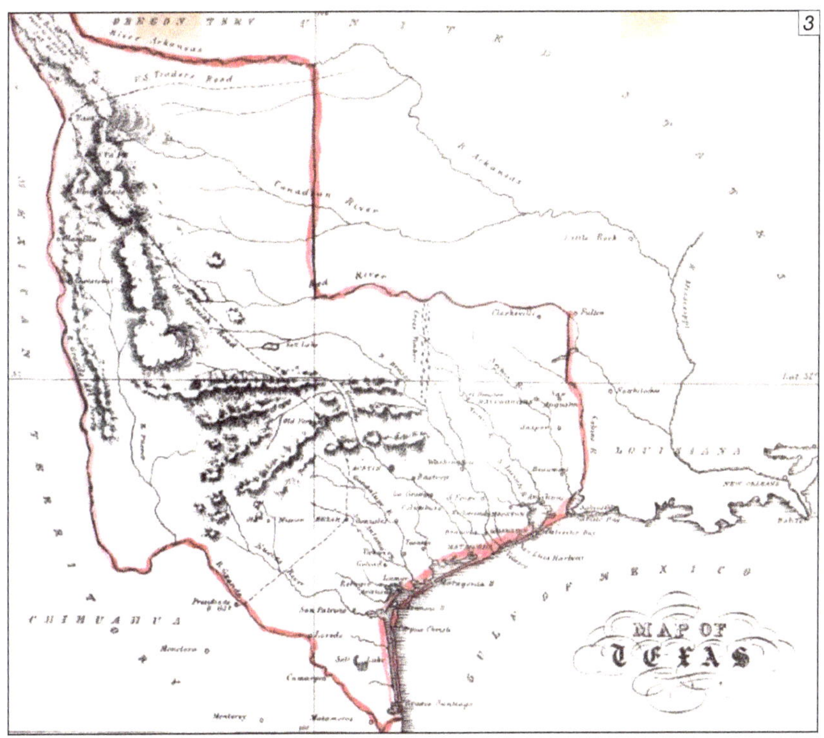

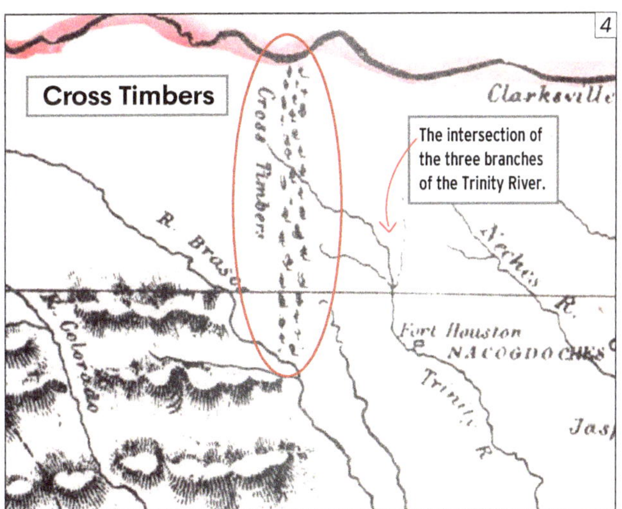

Figures 3 and 4: This map of Texas with natural features and cities was drawn by Arthur Ikin in 1841. The scale is not accurate, particularly in the western part of the state. In the close view (below) of North Central Texas, we see that neither Dallas nor Fort Worth are shown, but the Cross Timbers is depicted as a vertical barrier crossing the Elm Fork of the Trinity River. Map of Texas, 1841, by Arthur Ikin, Rare Book and Texana Collections, UNT Libraries, G4030 1841.I34 1841a.

The Cross Timbers was not a romantic, beautiful, or livable forest. It consisted of gnarled, interweaving trees such as Post Oaks and Blackjack Oaks with an understory of prickly vines and shrubs. The nature of the growth in the Cross Timbers made it difficult and painful to traverse. Branches snagged clothing and hair and scratched skin. Progress was slow as people hacked through saplings. Fever and insects were bothersome. American author and traveler Washington Irving compared it to fighting through trees of cast iron. It was therefore seen as a significant barrier, formidable and perhaps ominous. An animal seeking to escape the hunter could hide there. A criminal evading the forces of the law might do so as well, but it was otherwise unwelcoming. For those in early Dallas, it would have been the natural westward boundary of potential growth. It eventually fell to the axes of settlers harvesting wood. When fire was the only fuel for heating and cooking, it was valuable at home and as a commodity for sale to others.

In contrast, the Medical District lands northeast of the river did not support many trees. This was the Blackland Prairie, where soil heavy with clay supported the growth of wild grasses. Later pioneers would plow those grasses under so that the black soil could grow food crops and cotton. Little and Big Bluestem, Buffalo grass, and Switchgrass teamed with animal and insect life. Cottontail rabbits, antelope, deer, bears, wolves and perhaps even buffalo made the prairie and the edge

Figure 5: Prairie grasses such as the Switchgrass pictured here grew tall enough for animals to hide and did not resemble modern domestic grasses. Courtesy of Cattle Raisers Museum.

of the Cross Timbers their home. In 1890, the jawbone of a mastodon was uncovered along Maple Avenue. Can we imagine them running down the path of Harry Hines? Birds also nested on the prairie and in the floodplain, including Bobwhite Quail, Sage Grouse, Pheasant, Meadowlark and Field Sparrow. They had to be wary of the prowling Red Fox, hungry black bear, and other predators.

The plants, animals, and availability of water made the area attractive to Native Americans. Very small prehistoric settlements near the Cross Timbers existed from 860 to 1600s, and people were likely

Trinity River and the Three Forks of the Trinity River

by Robert Prejean

*A Mississippi River it is not;
however, the Trinity River can hold its own
among the Lone Star State's numerous rivers.
From its western headwaters of rolling prairies in
Archer County downstream to the Gulf Coast marshes
surrounding Galveston Bay in Chambers County,
the river's beauty is appreciated in the various physical
features it flows through. Yet, it is a river that has carried
several names and its watershed has drawn people
looking for opportunity and a new life.*

So, what's with the Trinity River's name? What we know today as the Trinity River has varied over time. The Texas State Historical Association notes that Caddo Indians referred to the river as Arkikosa in north central Texas, while Native Americans living along the Gulf Coast called it Daycoa. In 1687, one of the earliest European explorers, the famous French explorer Réne Robert Cavelier, Sieur de La Salle, called it *Riviere des canoës* (River of the Canoes) during his ill-fated expedition to establish a fort and colony along the Mississippi River. In 1690, Spanish explorer Alonso De León named the river *La Santisima Trinidad* (The Most Holy Trinity) while leading an expedition to secure Spanish claims to this countryside and rid it of French invaders.

Almost 150 years later, with Americans encroaching into the Gulf Coastal region of what would one day be Texas, the river's name got shortened with an English translation to simply the Trinity River.

Spanish explorer Alonso De León never came close to what is today's North Texas, so it is doubtful he was aware of the streams and forks on the upper Trinity River watershed when giving the river its Spanish name. As noted by John Henry Brown in his book *History of Dallas County, Texas, From 1837 To 1887*, the upper reaches of the Trinity River were still considered a wilderness to most:

This more immediate section, though occasionally traversed by adventurous hunters and trappers, was simply known by the people elsewhere by the somewhat appropriate designation of the "Three Forks of the Trinity" country, the Elm and Main forks uniting near Dallas and the Bois d'Arc or East fork about thirty miles below.

Prior to his known work as America's earliest landscape architect, Frederick Law Olmsted was a writer for the *New York Daily Tribune* who traveled into Texas between 1853 and 1854 to report on this southern state prior to the Civil War. His letters collected in the book, *A Journey through Texas, Or a Saddle-Trip on the Southwestern Frontier*, documents his experiences and assessments of Texas, its people, and its land, including his time crossing the Trinity River.

These bottom lands bordering the Trinity are among the richest of rich Texas. They are not considered equal, in degree of fatness, to some parts of the Brazos, Colorado, and Guadalupe bottoms, but are thought to have compensation in reliability for steady cropping. The open coast-prairie grazing districts extend to within a short distance of where we crossed. Above are some fine planting counties, and high up, in the region of the Forks of the Trinity are lands equally suitable to cotton, wheat, and corn, which were universally described to us as, for Southern settlers, the most promising part of the state.

Today, the Three Forks of the Trinity is now the location for one of most diverse economic regions in the nation and the country's fourth largest metropolitan area, home to 7.6 million residents that now call the Dallas-Fort Worth area home.

attracted to the banks of the river as well. This is called the late prehistoric period when arrow points began to appear. Their evolving shapes and some surviving fragments of Nocona Plain ceramics suggest the influence of southern plains tribes. The people also left traces of early agriculture and bison hunting. Investigations of settlements from this period at Joe Pool Lake uncovered remnants of corn roasting, so these northern settlements may have also grown corn.

Figure 6: A male and female Bobwhite Quail. Though often called the "Northern" or "Virginia" quail, Colinus virginianus was quite common in Texas. Courtesy of Cornell University Library.

In the Protohistoric period, 1600 to 1800, several tribes may have used the area, but probably not for permanent settlement. Tribes include the Tonkawa, Wichita, and Caddo. The Caddo commonly inhabited the eastern parts of northern Texas, where they built large settlements and left burial mounds, but their area ranged to the edge of Dallas County. They hunted game, traded with Europeans, and practiced some agriculture. The Keechi tribe of the Caddoan language family built a village along Cedar Springs Creek. It would have included the usual Caddo home, a rounded conical structure made of wood and soft natural covering.

Unfortunately, most potential archeological sites in and around the Medical District are not available for exploration. The key sites along the river were disrupted when the Trinity was rerouted in the early 20th century. Other sites may have been buried beneath hospital, industrial, and residential development

Figure 7: The Sage Grouse or Greater Prairie-Chicken were once common in Texas but were decimated during the 20th century. They are not extinct. Much of the decline is due to habitat loss, but they are also cursed with the misfortune of being reputedly tasty. This illustration is from a 1902 book entitled Birds that Hunt and are Hunted. Courtesy of the Biodiversity Heritage Library.

before anyone realized what was being lost. There was one rich store of artifacts found near the Medical District. Alvah White was working at his family's sand deposit near the original juncture of the Elm and West

Figure 8: The Sage Grouse and the other birds and small animals understood that the Red Fox was a serious hunter and constant threat. Courtesy of the Smithsonian Libraries.

forks of the Trinity River when he found an arrowhead. That first one appeared in the early 1950s. By 1961, the pile of sand had been flattened and over 300 arrowheads found. Mr. White consulted with experts who identified them as coming from several tribes. Evidence of actual settlement was not found. *The Dallas Morning News* suggested that "Dallas has long been considered a convention center," and that this was evidence of an early place of meeting.[3]

By 1800, Native American tribes from states to the east of Texas were being displaced, and some headed west. People of the Delaware, Chickasaw, Waco, Cherokee, and Shawnee tribes passed through the area in the 1830s. Skirmishes among these tribes and the existing tribes were frequent. By the 1840s, encroaching pioneer settlement pushed most tribes even further west.

Two interesting and very different tribes may have seen the Medical District area in

Figure 9: The Great Egret, which would have little to fear from a small fox, can still enjoy the Medical District. They nest each year in the bird rookery on the grounds of UT Southwestern's South Campus. They can be seen flying among the buildings. Courtesy of Paula Mason Photography.

those final years before American occupation of Dallas intruded. The Comanche maintained their independence, and the control of the lands they roamed, through fierce defiance and the skilled use of weapons and horses. They traded with first the Spanish and then the

---

3   Dinger, Griff, "Sand Hill Gives up Varied Indian Relics," in *The Dallas Morning News*, March 18, 1961, p. 1.

CHAPTER 1

Mexican rulers of Texas without surrendering their freedom, which they maintained long into the 1800s until the American push to the west became irresistible.

Their territory, their "Comancheria," stretched from Texas to Colorado. Other tribes within it feared them. The tribe included many groups. Texas Comanche belonged to the Nokoni band. Its most famous members are the leader of the band, Peta Nocona, his wife Cynthia Ann Parker (called Naduah among the Comanche), and their son Quanah Parker. When the Comanche raided Fort Parker in 1836, they took five captives,

Figure 10: These buffalo were photographed in 1932, grazing in an unknown location. Dallas was too urbanized by that time to still attract such herds, but they must have once looked just like this while dining on the prairie grasses of Dallas County. Courtesy of Schreiner University.

including eleven-year-old Cynthia Ann. She learned their language and ways of life, and she married Peta Nocona. The Red River town of Nocona, Texas, and its famous boots are named for him. A very large man, and a brave warrior, he may have led the raid on Fort Parker. When he was presumably lost at the Battle of Pease River in 1860, she wept for him and went into mourning. In that battle, the Texas Rangers rescued Cynthia Ann, though she might have disputed the term. She and her daughter Prairie Flower went to the home of her uncle, Colonel Isaac Parker, in Birdville. She never readjusted to American life, disliking the clothing, housing, and food, and mourning her lost husband and the two sons from whom she was separated. Prairie Flower died in 1864. In 1871, Cynthia Ann died after a period of depression during which she refused food and water.

That same year, her oldest son Quanah led his own band of Comanche in the Red River War and rose to a high leadership position. The U.S. government saw him as the chief of the Comanche and engaged him in making peace and moving the people to reservation lands in Oklahoma. He recognized that the days of Comanche warrior resistance to intruders had ended and surrendered in 1875.

The early Comanche constantly moved among all parts of their Comancheria and could have visited the lands of the Medical District. If so, they would have been a frightening visitor to the more peaceful

Alvah White's collection . . . hint of city's past.

TRINITY BOTTOMS

Sand Hill Gives Up Varied Indian Relics

By GRIFF SINGER

To say that the average Indian lorist is envious of Alvah White might be a gross understatement. His arrowhead collection numbers more than 300 and represents many tribes that once inhabited Texas.

But that's not the half of it. Over the past eight years, White hasn't bothered with a pick and shovel in his collecting. And he hasn't had to travel the width and breadth of the state.

The 26-year-old Irving man employed a dragline over a ½-mile area in the Trinity River lowlands north of the 4000-4200 block of Irving Boulevard to filter artifacts out of a sand hill that has since been removed for industrial structures.

White confides that his interest in Indian lore started by chance after he went to work in 1962 for an older brother in the J. C. White Sand Co.

"One day I looked down into a bucket of sand and spied an arrowhead, and I've been looking at the ground ever since," said the muscular White.

White and his family moved into the lowlands area in 1941 with his father farming 1,500 acres. Some years later the elder brother began taking sand from the big deposit near the original meeting of the West and Elm forks of the Trinity.

After more than 10 years of excavation, the big sand hill finally was leveled just more than a year ago.

Dallas has long been considered a convention center, and White believes therein lies the tale of his varied arrowhead collection.

"We're pretty sure the sand hill was surrounded by timber and provided a good camping spot," he commented. "We haven't found any evidences of permanent buildings in the area.

"One expert tells me the arrowheads represent many tribes, some from as far away as the Pecos area. So this must have been a meeting place or a popular battleground," he said.

And there are hints that the spot could have been the scene of fighting. Included with his collection of arrowheads—of many shapes and ranging from smaller than a dime to axe-head in size—are two cavalry spurs and a broken saber blade.

Figure 11: Mr. Alvah White with some of his archeological finds. Courtesy of The Dallas Morning News.

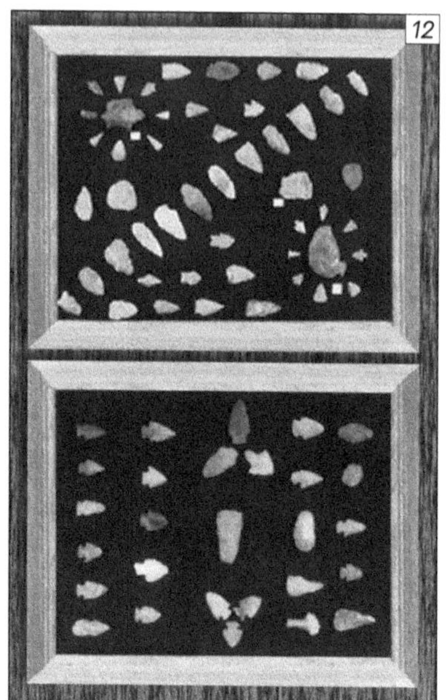

Figure 12: Arrowhead collectors like Ron Queen of Mineral Wells soon learn that they were made in a variety of shapes and sizes. Experts can often determine the source tribe by such clues, which help to trace the travels and trading activities of the makers. Like Alvah White, people digging for non-historic reasons can find themselves accidental archeologists when unexpected artifacts emerge from the ground. Courtesy of Tarrant County College Northeast, Heritage Room.

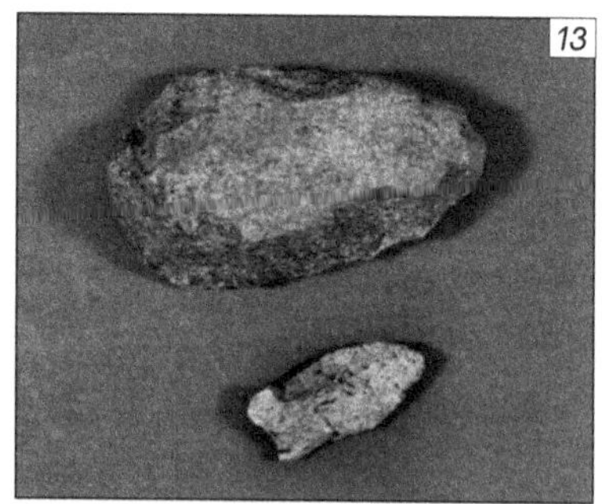

Figure 13: The scraper tool and arrowhead were found at a construction site in Coppell. Courtesy of Tarrant County College Northeast, Heritage Room.

tribes who frequented the area. And they might have even met a much different tribe from the east, the Cherokee, on their way to Indian Territory in Oklahoma.

The Cherokee tribe contrasted with Comanche by earlier adoption

Figure 14: The date of this photograph is unknown, but it clearly shows us Quanah Parker in his prime. Courtesy of Tarrant County College Northeast, Heritage Room.

of American ways of life, world-view, and political systems. This tactic did not protect them as hoped. Native to the southeastern part of the United States, in the early 1800s they retained some of their original territory in Georgia and tried to live as the Americans around them did. They built American style houses and embraced agriculture. They emulated American local political forms and created an alphabet to publish a newspaper in their language. None of these efforts at assimilation helped when

neighbors coveted their land. The famous Trail of Tears of 1838 was the forced relocation of the Cherokee to Oklahoma, with all that they had built in the east forfeited.

In Texas, hostilities between the Comanche, and the Spanish, Mexicans and then Texans raged from 1820 to 1875. The Comanche were seen by all of these governments as an impediment to northern settlement. Mexican officials tolerated the settlement of early Cherokee refugees in northeastern Texas as

Figure 15: This image, circa 1890, depicts an older Chief Parker on the porch of a house in Indian Territory. Courtesy of Clay County Historical Society, Inc.

potential allies in fighting more hostile tribes. The Republic of Texas initially maintained friendly relations, but under the presidency of Mirabeau Lamar, they deteriorated. Cherokee resistance failed and they were forced north of the Red River.

By the 1840s, the free reign of the Comanche and the travels of the Cherokee ended in the Dallas area. In the Medical District, the plants and animals, the river, and the prairie welcomed a new wave of human residents: the pioneers. The land would never look the same.

Figure 16: This beaded leather sacred pipe bag belonged to Quanah Parker and was a ceremonial object. Courtesy of the Dallas Historical Society.

FRONTIER SETTLEMENT IN THE DISTRICT

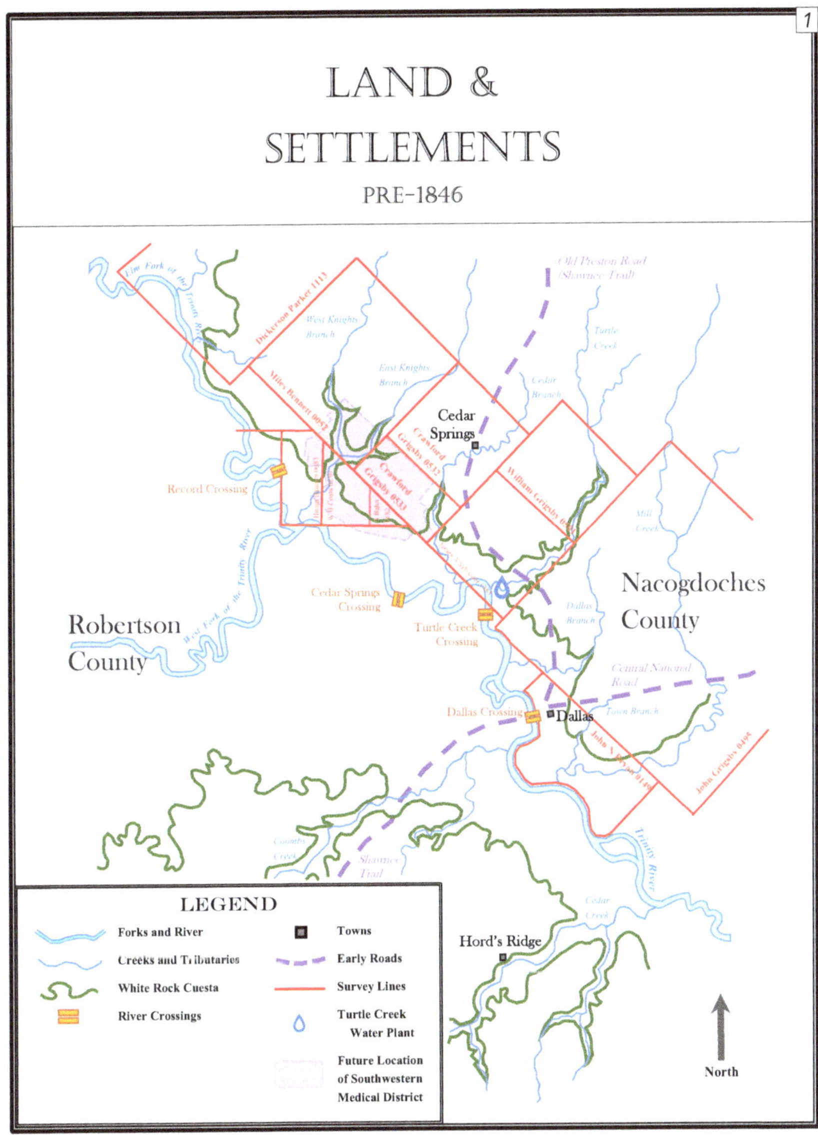

Figure 1: Map of the land grant divisions and other features of the area during the pioneer period. Courtesy of Robert Prejean.

The Native Americans lived more lightly on the land than the newcomers who arrived after 1840. They were ready to travel or rebuild in the event that rising waters overtook the Elm Fork floodplain and temporarily displaced them. Their agricultural efforts were limited to subsistence, so it did not matter if some of the soil in the Medical District was not useful for growing crops. They had traditional paths, often shared with migratory animals, that met their travel needs. This situation was not as attractive to potential immigrants who wanted to build permanent structures, or grow crops on a mass scale and ship them easily out of the area.

The early Spanish and Mexican governments were not interested in settling the Dallas area. Leaders of the Republic of Texas wanted to encourage Texans, Americans, and Europeans to occupy all the available lands, a recruiting effort that proved difficult. The Texas Emigration and Land Company was granted land for distribution in the north central part of the new nation. The company is commonly known as the Peters Colony after its founder, W. S Peters of Louisville, Kentucky.

Figures 2 and 3 (next page): This survey map depicts Dallas, Tarrant, and parts of Ellis County and Peters Colony land in 1853. The city of Dallas is on the upper right. Clearly, the lands of Dallas County were not yet as fully claimed as the lands to the west. Courtesy of The Texas General Land Office.

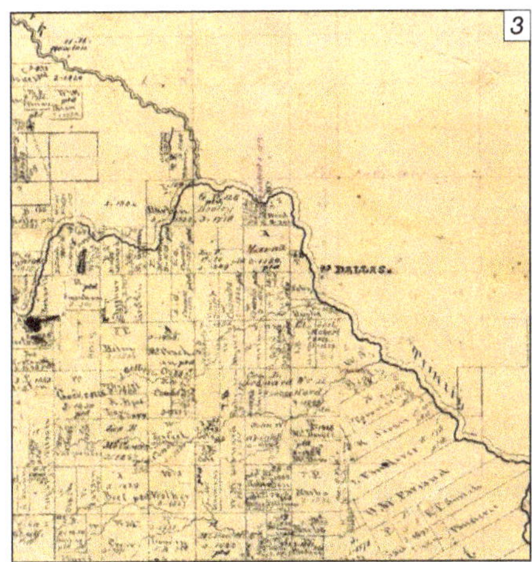

Figure 3: Survey map from Figure 2, zoomed in to Dallas.

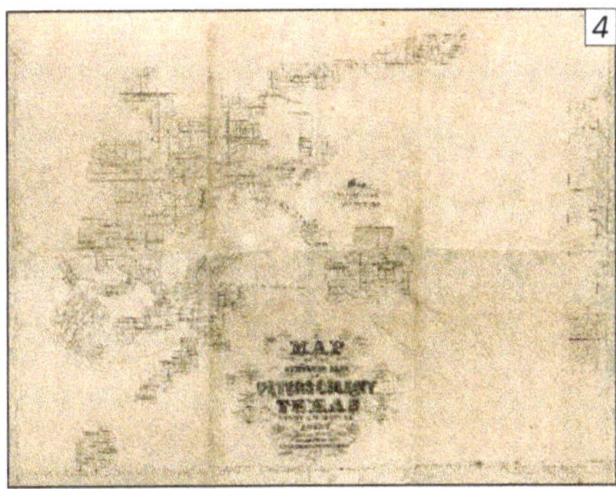

Figure 4: Five years later, in 1858, Henry Hedgcoxe drew this map of "the surveyed part of Peters Colony." It barely reaches the western edge of Fort Worth on the right. Dallas is not included, but once again, the western counties appear to be a priority.

They were awarded land in four contracts; the later ones included the Medical District. The first contract, 1841, started at the Red River and went south to the northern border of Dallas County. The second contract, later in 1841, expanded south to include part of western Dallas County, including some of the Medical District. The 1842 third contract included most of the county and all of the Medical District. The grants awarded 640 acres per family if the claimants lived and worked on the land, so the intent was to build lasting settlements.

Mismanagement and scandal plagued the organization, at one point inspiring the colonists to rise up against the local representative in the "Hedgcoxe War." Mr. Henry Hedgcoxe was lucky to escape the raid on his office with his life and some of his business papers. People were left with confusing or missing records of their land awards that took years to resolve. The Peters Colony was not as efficient or honest as they could have been, but they did contribute many early residents to the area.

Much of the land in the Medical District was really not available for settlement via the Peters Colony. It had already been given by the Republic to soldiers in the Texas Revolution as a reward. A large piece went to Miles Bennett (1816-1887). He fought at the Battle of Gonzales and was rewarded with a land grant of 1/3 of a league of land (1,476 acres) in Nacogdoches County, which at that time extended to Dallas.

His piece of Texas is shaped like a diamond on a map, with points to the cardinal directions. This is the mark of Dallas' most famous pioneer surveyor, Warren Angus Ferris. He used the Spanish tradition, based on the Laws of the Indies, while he was the surveyor for Nacogdoches County in the early years of the Republic of Texas. In that system, property lines run 45 degrees to the compass points. Other surveyors used the American system of grid lines running to the compass points. The inevitable result of this dual system was awkwardly triangular pieces of land and later streets that collide at 45-degree angles.

In 1841, Ferris surveyed a line of Republic of Texas land grants running from southeast of downtown to the northwest. Past downtown, the grants begin with that of John Grigsby, through lands of his sons to Miles Bennett's and Dickenson Parker's. Those of Bennett and Crawford Grigsby contain most of the Medical District. UT Southwestern North Campus and student housing and the northern UT Dallas facility are within the Bennett Survey.[1]

Bennett never lived in Dallas, spending his later years in Anderson County.[2] His family must have visited Dallas at some point, because his sister Elizabeth met and married Dallas pioneer William Grigsby. That family's patriarch, John Grigsby, lived in Houston and drowned before he could visit Dallas to see the "league and labor" (4,428 acres plus 177) granted to him for his revolutionary service. John Grigsby's land makes up most of what is now downtown Dallas, and rather crowded in on the lands and city plan of city founder John Neely Bryan. His claim lay between the survey border and the riverbank. It was William and his brother Crawford who came to Dallas, where Crawford participated in the surveying of the land in 1841. John Grigsby left many heirs from two marriages. His second wife's subsequent marriage, death, and spouse's remarriage within the family made for a complicated family tree and lawsuits in the 1870s about the division of the land.

Bennett sold some of his land early and retained some for years. His absentee landownership may have contributed to the slow rate

----

1   Much information about this plot of land has been assembled in a report from Geo-Marine, Inc. that UTSW commissioned as part of their due diligence before beginning construction. See Duane E. Peter, Donna Shepard and Steven M. Hunt, *An Evaluation of the Potential Presence of Historic Properties Located Within the North Campus Expansion Area of the University of Texas Southwestern Medical Center*, Dallas, Texas, Miscellaneous Report of Investigations Number 64, Geo-Marine, Inc., 1993.

2   Given his geographic diversity of land holdings, Bennett is of interest to local historians in both Dallas and Anderson Counties. See "John Grigsby Survey Records," in *The Quarterly*, 24, 2, June 1978, p. 79; and "Statement of Mrs. Laura Bennett-Taken down by Kate Hunter, June 19, 1923," in *The Tracings*, 14, 2, July 1995, pp. 9-12.

of permanent settlement near the intersection of Inwood and Harry Hines. Such ownership leads to tenant farming and does not promote lasting settlement and commitment to the location. Though not really a Dallasite, Bennett's name lives on in the county every time a piece of land from his survey is sold, because the legal description of the property includes "Miles Bennett Survey" and always will.

John Neely Bryan showed no interest in the lands of the Medical District. He arrived in 1841 to build a trading post. Discovering that potential settlement was beginning, he changed course and founded the town of Dallas at his chosen spot on the Trinity River, near the current location of the Triple Underpass. Bryan was clearly wise in the ways of travel and trade. His location was along the traditional travel routes of the Native Americans he planned to trade with, and right at the best place to cross the Trinity. There were other places to cross the river. Three were in or near the Medical District: Cedar Springs Crossing, Record Crossing, and Turtle Creek Crossing. None were as usable as the Dallas Crossing at Bryan's settlement.

The course of city settlement was determined by the land and the water. Dallas is crossed by the White Rock Cuesta, a cuesta being a ridge sloped on one side and steep on the other. The steep side in this case faces west and discourages travel. The White Rock Cuesta passes from the southwest corner of the county to Bryan's chosen site, where the Trinity cut through it, and then continues northwest and north, somewhat overlapping the Medical District. The cuesta is Austin Chalk Limestone and Eagle Ford Shale, contributing to the soil content of the area. The easiest place to cross the Trinity is where it cuts the cuesta, and so Bryan settled there. Near downtown, the floodplain is only a mile wide, but on the Elm Fork, it is five miles wide, a large swath of land inhospitable to lasting settlement. In that strip of land, the river enriches the soil but poses a constant threat. The Elm Fork was difficult to cross. Bryan's dreams of using the Trinity for shipping goods were misguided. The river is hard to navigate, and often runs low. Unfortunately, it can also run quite high, flooding areas from downtown eastward, leading to its relocation beginning in 1928. Nonetheless, Bryan chose his river location for a city well, as it was destined to be the focus of land transportation.

The earliest roads that were established through Dallas confirmed the wisdom of his choice. The Old Preston Road was completed in

1843. It ran from Austin to Coffee's trading post on the Red River, north of Sherman. Much of this new road followed established Native American trails. A short-lived military post was established along it, possibly the first structure built in Dallas County by anyone other than Native Americans. The road used the convenient Trinity crossing at Bryan's settlement, and then continued north. It came tantalizingly close to the Medical District, without reaching into its lands. In 1844, surveying began for the Central National Road of the Republic of Texas. It was to begin in Dallas County and extend to the northeast to the Red River.[3] Not surprisingly, the road started at Bryan's settlement and went east, with no relation to the Medical District. Both roads were intended to ease travel for settlers and the movement of agricultural and manufactured goods and gave the most benefit to places near their routes.

Figures 5 and 6: Cities along the route of the Shawnee Trail display bronze sculptures of running longhorns and the cowboys who drove them, all larger than actual size. They run along a man-made water feature, adjacent to the Pioneer Park Cemetery where many early Dallas pioneers are buried. Bronze figures by Robert Summers in Pioneer Plaza, Texas Trees Foundation.

---

3   For a full explanation of how these and other Texas roads came to be, see J. W. Williams, *Old Texas Trails*, Kenneth F. Neighbours, ed., (Burnet, TX.: Eakin Press, 1979).

Need Directions?

by Robert Prejean

Driving in and around the streets of Dallas might seem confusing, perhaps illogical, or of another dimension. Streets seem to cross at 45 degree angles to one another. An east-west road suddenly becomes northeast-southwest, and when entering downtown Dallas' street grid, be ready to take one turn followed blocks later by yet still another. The sun rises in the east and sets in the west but asking for simple directions usually provides no guiding light. Your mind is spinning, and you almost hear the voice of Rod Serling saying, "Your next stop, the Twilight Zone."

Hiding under your bed covers won't help, but a bird's-eye view plus a little understanding of how Dallas County was surveyed will ease your nerves plus provide some insight on why Dallas streets ended up being the way they are. These surveys were developed before and after the formation of Dallas County, and when created, each seemed logical for the purpose intended. The surveys reflect a 16th century Spanish crown decree for town planning, a frontier trader establishing his post at a river crossing, plus basic American land opportunism.

Two excellent books help explain Dallas' survey patterns and street grid riddle. One is *Land is the Cry!* by Dallas historian and writer Susanne Starling, while the second is *A Field Guide to American Houses* by the late Virginia Savage McAlester of Dallas. Starling's book is a well-documented account of Warren Angus Ferris, a Nacogdoches County surveyor during the Republic of Texas when the County once extended into portions of today's Dallas County and locations east. Ferris visited the area known as the Three Forks of the Trinity River and was the first to survey what is now Dallas County, several years before John Neely Bryan built his cabin and surveyed the original town site of Dallas. Arriving in Texas after its independence from Mexico, Ferris soon became the Nacogdoches County surveyor. New to the job but attune to the demands, Ferris' surveying technique followed the influence of the Laws of the Indies—by decree from the Spanish crown, it provided instructions on town planning in the New World such that sunlight reach all rooms of a building plus the need for air circulation.

Surveying at 45 degrees to a cardinal point addressed such needs for human habitation. Ferris' surveying can be seen in the roads that followed survey lines making up portions of Dallas, Hunt, Kaufman, Rockwall, and Van Zandt Counties, all once part of Nacogdoches County.

This placement of early survey lines was noted further in McAlester's book, which is primarily a comprehensive guide to domestic architecture. A section in the book about neighborhoods and the impact of early surveys focused on the three distinct survey patterns that have to this day influenced Dallas' thoroughfares, street grids, land use and zoning patterns, plus neighborhood character on the north side of the Trinity River. As seen from above, most notable in the older sections of Dallas is the 45 degree angle of local streets stretching from the Bachman Lake area on the northwest to Fair Park and South Dallas on the southeast. This reflects the survey work of Ferris and the lingering influence of 16th century Spanish royalty in North Texas.

A second survey pattern creates an odd 14 degree east-west gouge encroaching into the earlier survey. This change to Dallas streets resulted from the handiwork of Dallas founder and trader John Neely Bryan in 1841. McAlester wrote that Bryan laid out the town's original street grid to correspond to the bend in the Trinity River at the most favorable crossing of the river. Bryan's town site was just outside Ferris' original survey lines, which didn't always extend to the riverbank. Nevertheless, the town site's principal streets of Commerce, Main, and Elm Streets continued their straight path almost two-miles into the Ferris' adjoining survey. The third and final impact to surveying Dallas County occurred soon after Texas joined the United States, as survey lines for the remainder of the County followed the established American surveying of subdividing the wilderness east to west and north to south plus some river long-lot surveys.

So, the next time you anxiously wander the streets of Dallas, gripping the steering wheel, seeing nothing but red, slowly looking over your shoulder and thinking you're losing your mind...your next stop, a Road Construction Zone.

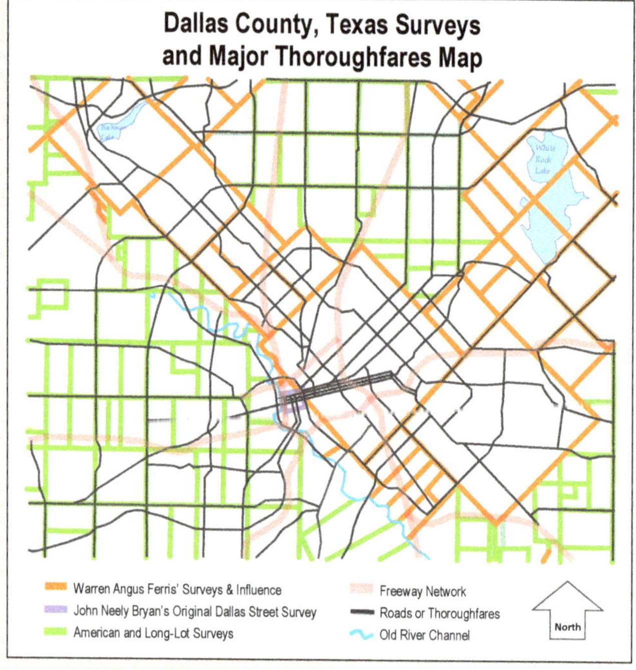

NEED DIRECTIONS?

Another type of Texas transportation route briefly ran through Dallas and along the edge of the Medical District. In the case of the Shawnee Trail, the term "ran" was literal for the northbound cattle. The trail crossed the Trinity downtown and followed the general route of the Old Preston Road to Cedar Springs. As the cattle drivers led their charges in that direction, how many of those stubborn creatures may have visited the lands of the Medical District? We can envision them enjoying the tasty prairie grasses before the pioneer farmers arrived. The Longhorns may have grazed some of the same places as the buffalo once did, places that now host hospitals.

By the 1850s, Texas Longhorns became less welcome in other states due to the Texas Fever transmitted by ticks they carried. Yet the drives carried on. The Shawnee Trail was one of the earliest, and the furthest east. It was busiest for the periods before and after the cattle drive hiatus of the Civil War. After that, the trails further west were preferred as more convenient. They continued in use to the late 1800s. Fort Worth became Cowtown and Dallas moved on to other sources of wealth but commemorated the trail in the Longhorn sculptures gathered at Pioneer Plaza downtown.

CEDAR SPRINGS AND THE COLE FAMILY

The Cedar Branch and the Cedar Springs gave their name to an early settlement that challenged the tiny settlement of Dallas for county leadership and lost. A location near a waterway was desirable to all pioneers trying to build a community. The challenge was to enjoy the benefits of fresh water, a flow that could support the turning of a wheel to power an engine or transportation by boat, while not suffering the perils of flooding.[4]

Unlike Bryan's Dallas, the town of Cedar Springs had no dreams of water transportation and little fear of flooding. They were able to operate a mill with the power of the Cedar Branch, and fresh spring water was always a benefit. The town and its namesake road do not really reach into the Medical District. However, it served as the earliest outpost of settlement interest in that Dallas quadrant. It gave rise to Oak Lawn, the main area to draw Dallasites west when the city became more urban.

---

4   For more on the story of Cedar Springs, with charming illustrations by Barbara Whitehead, see A. C. Greene, *A Town Called Cedar Springs*, 1984.

Miss Eleanor Winn and the Maple Hill School

by Robert Prejean

A one-room schoolhouse and a teacher. A schoolhouse is nothing more than a structure, but it becomes a place of learning for opening minds depending on the instructor. In four short years, Miss Eleanor Winn, the Dallas teacher and superintendent of the Maple Hill School, left a lasting, positive influence in the lives of nomadic families and their children, people that had long been ignored.

Who was Eleanor Winn?

Eleanor M. Winn was the second oldest of six children of the late Thomas Winn and Anna Margaret Winn. Eleanor, also known as Ella, was born on August 5, 1857, in Chillicothe, Ohio, a city forty-five miles south of Columbus, the current capital of Ohio. Chillicothe's claim to fame is that it served as the first and third capital of Ohio.

In a June 5, 1927 *Dallas Morning News* interview with Eleanor Winn, she described Chillicothe as "a beautiful little town devoted to education and culture." The same article noted she graduated at age ten and went on to receive her teacher training by Dr. John Hancock, superintendent of Chillicothe schools. Dr. Hancock would later serve as State Superintendent of Ohio schools and Cincinnati schools.

Eleanor's older sister Jane and younger sister Theresa were also teachers in Chillicothe's schools, although Jane would later move to St. Louis, and through her journalistic writings and pen name Frank Fair would become known as "the dean of newspaper women." Theresa eventually moved to Dallas to teach primary elementary pupils. In the late 1890s, Eleanor spent summers teaching at a teachers' college in Boulder, Colorado, while being active in the local Chautauqua camp.

Considering the old myth that a woman never tells her age, Eleanor had some fun taking this to a new level, even with the census takers. For the 1900 Census, she reported her birth year as 1865 and age 35, then in the 1920 Census gave her birth year as 1885 and age 35. Throughout her life she remained single but kept active and involved. During a 1912 holiday visit with family members in St. Louis, she attended a rally for the woman's suffrage and returning to Dallas advocated women's right to vote "to have a voice in the settling of all public questions at the ballot, its proper place."

Lured to Texas

It was in Boulder when then Dallas public schools' superintendent J.L. Long met Eleanor and asked her to come to Dallas to teach where her younger sister Theresa was already a teacher. *The News* article noted that following the

1899 close of the Boulder Chautauqua camp, Eleanor Winn returned briefly to Chillicothe, Ohio; however, the thought of teaching in Texas took over.

The following October, she settled for several years in Dallas to be a member of the teaching staff of both the Cumberland Hill School and Fannin School. A *Dallas Morning News* story noted that from 1907 to 1909, Eleanor Winn was appointed primary supervisor at Houston, but resigned to accept a position as feature writer and society editor at *The Dallas Morning News* before returning for good as a teacher in the Dallas schools.

Woodchuck Hill and the Maple Hill School

Driving along Maple Avenue past the well-tended campus of Scottish Rite for Children Orthopedics Hospital or the wooded hills of Reverchon Park where people play and walk their dogs, you would never suspect that this area once had a different reputation, a different name, and for a short time, a one-room schoolhouse. Once known as Woodchuck Hill, this area on the edge of Dallas had an unsavory reputation of squatter camps, people in poor circumstances, unlawfulness, and people without roots. The latter were made up of proud but uneducated itinerant families following the season's crops in their wagons by picking cotton and berries plus chopping wood to make a living and feed a family.

Civic leaders at the time realized they had a problem and as noted in the May 24, 1929 *Dallas Morning News* story, "Dallas set about to reclaim people first, land next." The *News* article goes on to note, "Social workers, handicapped by the newness and lack of tested experience in their profession met conditions with even face. They were assisted by Miss Eleanor Winn whom the school board placed in charge of a little white schoolhouse on the hill."

The school opened in early 1911 with an initial enrollment of forty-two students with books donated by school Superintendent Professor Arthur Lefevre. Instead of a tent, a new one-room school building was built with four grades being taught. Eleanor Winn made sure lessons intermixed the three R's with outdoor learning. On sunny days, lessons would be conducted out in the open air on benches built by one of the boys. A May 5, 1911 *Dallas Morning News* article quoted Eleanor saying, "There isn't a tree in this flat which these children do not know all about. They know its habits and its use." The article went on to note the school also had a flower garden plus a vegetable garden producing watermelons, okra, onions, cucumbers, collards, tomatoes, corn, Irish potatoes, beans, peas, and radishes. The first fruit of radish was sent to Professor Lefevre, but the pupils enjoyed the rest with a radish party of crackers and salt. A local truck farmer purchased the remaining beans and peas.

August 26, 1911, Eleanor made a request for an adequate supply of water along with the addition of a small room for the children of the tent community to bathe since Woodchuck Hill lacked such facilities. The headline on page 6 of the May 7, 1912 *Dallas Morning News* boasted: "BATHTUB COURSE AT MAPLE HILL SCHOOL – Water and rag for each pupil who is enrolled." The school board had decided to build a small bathhouse that was finished in late February, complete with a turquoise blue painted tub with hot and cold water. Lining the walls around the tub were wet wash rags hung on nails, with each owner's name listed by the wash rag nail. From teacher to pupil, the one rule that had to be followed was, "No exchange of wash rags."

The bath house provided an added benefit as a social center to the tent community, particularly the use of hot water for families with small babies. A practical cook stove used to heat the water had many benefits from being a gathering place when the teacher gave a taffy pull for the children in winter months to various uses for cooking.

Maple Hill School began having visitors wanting to learn more about the school's nature-based setting and unique approach for teaching children of traveling families while still stressing the basics of reading, writing, and arithmetic. But it went beyond the simple basics. Teaching also extended to an appreciation for being polite, maintaining cleanliness, respecting one's natural surroundings, and learning poetry.

Teaching even extended to learning the tales of King Arthur and court of fair ladies and brave knights. As revealed in a May 5, 1912 *Dallas Morning News* article describing the school, the students took their studies seriously:

A little girl around seven years of age, described as "a little creature of a primitive civilization in the heart of a city" rose to impress a visitor and crossing her little bare feet told the tale of "The Fair Maid of Astolot" in her own words – "Launcelot was mean to her; she couldn't git him to wear her red sleeve at all when he wint off to fight. Then she got in a tug..." Over in a corner of the school room a little boy quietly raised his hand and corrected: "Miss Winn, it was a black barge." The little novice story teller went on acquiescing "in a barge, all dressed in a gold dress with lilies in her hand and the dumb man rowed her with a letter in his hand for Launcelot. They stopped at Camelot." The story brought the girls to tears and aroused one little boy to say, "Launcelot didn't have no right to treat that girl that way."

Eleanor Winn was a frequent speaker and instructor to teacher groups on topics such as "Reaching the Unreachable" and "The Individual in the Making." Besides her seventeen summers at Boulder, Eleanor taught in the following summer positions: three summers in the Normal Department of the University of Texas Summer School; one summer at Daniel Baker College, Brownwood; one at Harris County Normal; one at Denton Normal; two summers at Victoria; one summer at Terrell; one at Wichita Falls; and one summer in Otero County, Colorado.

The Maple Hill School lasted until 1915 when the city purchased Woodchuck Hill as a future site for Turtle Creek Park, later renamed Reverchon Park. Years later in a June 5, 1927 *Dallas Morning News* interview, Eleanor Winn recalled:

"I applied for and was given the place as teacher. Instead of a tent school, as was first planned, a neat building was erected, and there I taught for four years. The school was open to all. Men and women alike wrote on the blackboards and sat at the desks poring over simple lessons. Local welfare organizations, eleven in all, began intensive work in the community, and every effort was made to arouse a spirit of ambition in the residents to acquire better quarters. No coercion was used, but at the end of four years the entire settlement, having learned what better living meant, made a quiet exodus."

Shortly before Christmas in 1933, with the two sisters retired from teaching, they were surrounded by boys and girls from the Fannin School, where Theresa Winn taught for ten years, who paid them a Christmas visit, bearing a huge basket of candy and fruits and singing Christmas carols.

Thomas Winn, Anna Margaret Winn, and four of their six children were buried in Grandview Cemetery in Chillicothe, Ohio, while Eleanor and Theresa were buried at Restland Memorial Park in their adopted hometown of Dallas. Eleanor Winn passed away on February 9, 1935, due to pneumonia believed to be brought on by confinement from a broken leg suffered in December 1934. On August 2, 1937, Theresa Winn, who retired in 1933 due to poor health after forty years teaching mostly at Dallas' San Jacinto and James W. Fannin schools, departed earth. Theresa Winn's obituary in *The Dallas Morning News* noted there were no surviving relatives.

Mills were low-tech industrial machines. The power of the flowing water was captured by a turning wheel, which then became the engine for mechanical devices. The mill at Cedar Springs was a grist mill for grinding grain, built by William A. Gold and Dick Donaldson. They also opened a distillery on site, a profitable way to use grain. For a grist mill, the key component of the machine is the millstone, a carefully shaped large stone donut. It could transform raw grain grown by local farmers into usable flour for their subsistence. The millstone from Cedar Springs was made in France and brought to Dallas from New Orleans by William Terry Edmondson. His descendants donated it for display in Lakeside Park, along Turtle Creek in Highland Park.

The mill building no longer exists. Dr. John Cole and his family were the early pioneers of Cedar Springs. In 1843, they arrived from their Texas entry point on the Red River via Preston Road. So would many other settlers, who either stopped at Cedar Springs or continued on the road to Dallas or south of the Trinity. For many, Cedar Springs was like a rest stop for

Figure 7: "Grist for the Mill," a mural by Maxwell B. Campbell, depicts farmers bringing sacks of grain to the mill for grinding. Courtesy of the Dallas Public Library.

resupplying before moving on. The road did not tend to direct anybody to the area of the Medical District.

Dr. Cole was Dallas' first physician, but as a pioneer, he took up farming and ran a store. Doctoring was often a sideline in frontier places, but Dr. Cole did open a pharmacy as well. He purchased his 160 acres from John Grigsby. As the leader of the town, he put it forth as a candidate for county seat when Dallas County was organized in 1846. When the election was held four years later, the temporary seat, Dallas, beat both Cedar Springs and Hord's Ridge in modern Oak Cliff. Dr. Cole did not live long enough to see the election. If Cedar Springs had won, the Medical District might well have become part of downtown. The Cole family continued as civic leaders in Dallas as it grew.

OBADIAH KNIGHT

Dr. Cole's unofficial successor as the leading advocate of Cedar Springs was Obadiah Knight. Obadiah arrived in Dallas in 1846,

Figure 8: The millstone on display in Lakeside Park. Photograph by Robert Prejean.

joining his brother Gabriel who came the year before. They came from Tennessee. Obadiah led the people of Cedar Springs in the fight to win election as the county seat in 1850. When they lost to Dallas, he suspected Bryan of cheating.

While Gabriel declared that his central interest was hunting the county game, Obadiah concentrated on land ownership and building the city. His farm reached the size of 1,000 acres, extending from the town of Cedar Springs to Love Field, ending in the Medical District. His house was on Inwood Road, near Cedar Springs Road.

The earliest civic amenities at Cedar Springs, a school and church, were built on a corner of his land. The mill and the town's store were also there.

He profited from raising livestock and agricultural products. His descendants credited his success to frugality and hard work, which certainly may be true, but it must also be recognized that he arrived in Dallas with a large contingent of enslaved people. This proves that he was already well-off financially before he arrived, and that much of the hard work was not done by him.

Another pioneer near the Medical District was Col. George W. Record. He had very good luck in his Dallas land acquisition. He reached Dallas in 1853. His holdings along the old course of the Elm Fork, just west of the current hospitals, included a good point for those wanting to travel west. Wagons and animals were able to ford the river on a base of higher stone in the bed. It naturally became known as Record Crossing, a name that lives on as a road. The current road traverses the old path to the river crossing, but the river has moved a half a mile away.

When it still flowed, it provided a valuable resource for a pioneer settlement and income for Col. Record. In the mid-1850s, he and his

Gill Well

by Robert Prejean

If by the grace of the entertainment gods, J.R. Ewing could have traded places with Forrest Gump, his Texas momma would have advised him that drilling in Texas... "is like a box of chocolates. You never know what you're gonna get."

In the last decades of the 19th century, Dallas, like most North Central Texas cities with a County Seat and rail stop, was growing and in need of a reliable water supply for drinking water and fire safety. The 1890 Census listed Dallas as the largest city in Texas, and Dallas was becoming a rail, trade, and financial center in Texas. The abundance of water in Dallas as in Texas is a rollercoaster of way too much or little to be had. In 1894, fifty-five miles south of Dallas, the City of Corsicana drilled a well in search of a good and reliable source of water. Instead of water, the citizens of Corsicana ended up with Texas' first major oil discovery. Dallas' search for water would have its own turn of events.

Dallas was no stranger to wells. There was a well drilled near Browder Springs at City Park and another at the County Courthouse; however, these wells faced obstacles or were not deep enough. In the 1880s and 1890s, several test wells were drilled along Turtle Creek, but their flow was not enough to meet the needs. For a time, water for the city was pumped from the Trinity River, but Fort Worth's waste flowing down the West Fork of the Trinity River required a viable, quick alternative. The flow and proximity of nearby streams, small lakes, forks of the Trinity River, and known artesian wells were all under consideration. Some attempts were made to dam and capture flowing waters, but these were subjected to the ups and downs of Texas rainfall.

In the first years of the 20th century, city leaders embarked once again on a test well that would reach the Trinity Sands and what was considered a sea of water 2,600 to 2,800 feet below the streets of Dallas. This initial test well would become known as Gill Well in reference to the City Alderman and Water Commission Chair, Charles A. Gill. Boring of the well began in 1903 and its progress was noted in newspapers almost weekly. At 1,900 feet down, engineers reached a strong flow of approximately 1,000,000 gallons per day of mineral water. Drilling continued but with the mineral water separated from contaminating the desirable pure water being sought. With news of mineral water pouring forth, it was reported that hundreds of people would come daily with jugs to gather the curative waters.

By November 1904, drilling reached 2,586 feet with a flow rate of 600,000 gallons per day of pure sweet water, pressure of 120 pounds to the square inch, and water temperature of 100 degrees. But in early December, problems began while enlarging the well. Below 2,200 feet, the stratum was unstable and during reaming, a pipe broke. Later, drills got stuck and in February 1904, a joint of pipe estimated to be twenty to fifty feet long got stuck in the well. In the months that followed, various efforts were made to fish out the obstruction, but by August 1904, Alderman Gill notified the City Council in a resolution that work to remove the obstructions were unsuccessful and that work was stopped. In the resolution, he also resigned as Chair of the Water Commission, which the Council did not accept. Despite this setback and knowing what they did, in the years that followed, the city drilled other nearby wells that were successful.

While the mineral waters could not be allowed to flow in city mains, it was a resource to be exploited. In the 19th and early 20th centuries, people sought out hot mineral waters for their medicinal remedies for whatever ailed them. Seeing the value from Gill Well's warm free-flowing mineral water, civic leaders saw new opportunities from its medicinal qualities. Some envisioned hospitals or health resorts and sanitariums like those in French Lick, Indiana, Hot Springs, Arkansas, or even closer to home in Marlin or Mineral Wells, Texas. Others saw the value of a natatorium for year-round swimming. For city leaders, the waters were a public resource to be available at no cost to the citizenry.

In March 1905, residents of Oak Lawn petitioned for permission to have Gill Well mineral waters piped to the City (Parkland) Hospital at Maple and Oak Lawn Avenues. In the last months of 1905, the Gill Well Sanitarium Company reached an agreement with the city to use the mineral waters at its proposed bathhouse and natatorium and build a pipeline and pagoda to be sited at City Hospital where residents could collect Gill Well water for free.

The Gill Well Bathhouse opened in January 1907 and the pagoda on the summer of 1907. Both the pagoda and bathhouse's natatorium were popular places. The year-round warm waters at the natatorium became popular for both Campfire Girls and Boy Scouts. The scout master even urged all Boy Scouts to learn how to swim at the Gill Well Natatorium. A July 27, 1911, article in *The Dallas Morning News* reported during a meeting of the Dallas Board of Commissioners that this body approved plans and specifications for tuberculosis patients to have toilet and bath building built on hospital grounds using Gill Well mineral waters.

In less than two decades, both the bathhouse and pagoda were either removed or relocated. The bathhouse was torn down in the 1920s for road improvement efforts to eliminate the dangerous sloping Maple Avenue curve, straighten and lower Maple Avenue, plus install a railroad overpass. A 1930 Fairchild Survey aerial for this area

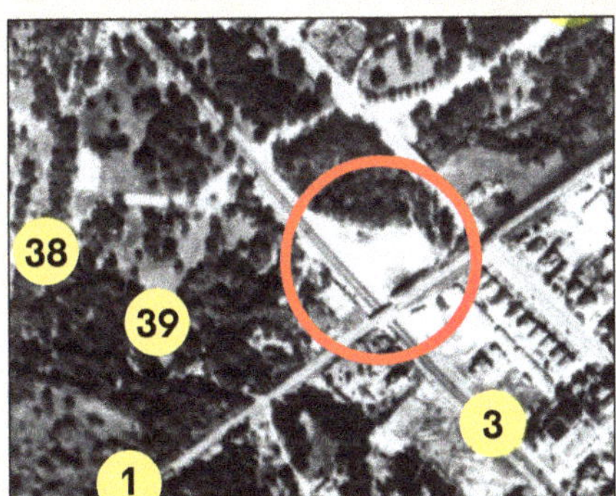

1930 Fairchild Survey aerial showing (within red circle) scar remnants of removed Maple Avenue curve and bluffs. Labeled features include: (1) Missouri, Kansas, and Texas (Katy) Railroad, (3) Maple Avenue, (38) Turtle Creek Boulevard, and (39) Reverchon Park. Source: Foscue Map Library, SMU, Dallas, TX, 1930 Fairchild Survey, Grid 51.

Source: The Dallas Morning News, December 1, 1903, page 10.

Source: The Dallas Morning News, January 13, 1907, page 21.

clearly shows the remaining scar of where the former curving Maple Avenue and adjacent bluffs once stood, today the site of a tennis court. The pagoda, becoming a traffic hazard, was moved further into the Parkland Hospital grounds in 1924.

Besides the Gill Well Bathhouse and Natatorium, others wanted to exploit the mineral waters and its curative qualities. In July 1905, *The Dallas Morning News* reported that the 150,000 Club, a civic group formed to attract big conventions and meetings to Dallas, wanted to promote Dallas as a health resort based on the medicinal qualities from Gill Well waters. Two years later, the newspaper carried an article that the Dallas Commercial Club issued a resolution supporting initiatives to make Dallas a health resort, complete with hotels and boarding houses, with the Gill Well Sanitarium Company site as an ideal location. In 1924, a business group submitted a proposal to build a health resort in conjunction with Reverchon Park plus seek Gill Well bottling rights from the city. Two years later, the Dallas Park Board received two proposals to build near Gill Well a sanitarium and bathhouse. One of the proposals sought to lease a portion of Reverchon Park to build a swimming pool, bathhouse, and eventually a hospital.

By the mid-20th century, interest in the Gill Well mineral waters waned. In March 1940, R.L. Johnson, one of the builders of the Gill Well Bathhouse, pitched his proposal to municipal leaders to build a year-round swimming and health center in exchange for the exclusive use of two "Gill wells" owned by the city. The health center and natatorium would be in proximity to the new Dallas high school stadium, later known as P.C. Cobb Stadium. Even though he posted the $100 deposit to secure the rights, the defense efforts of World War II put his plans on hold. On February 11, 1942, R.L. Johnson passed away at age 65, never seeing his plans come to reality.

On March 26, 1950, the Gill Well hydrant, now located along Oak Lawn across from the high school stadium, suddenly erupted, throwing mineral water twenty feet into the air. Those still alive who drilled the well in the first decade of the 20th century wondered if the lodged pipe that created the blockage had become unsealed, allowing the pressure of the waters from the Trinity Sands to gush upward.

Then after, the only closing note about the demise of Gill Well was a mention in Sam Acheson's June 22, 1970 *Dallas Morning News* article recalling

Where medicinal waters once flowed—shuttered stone fountain in Reverchon Park near Maple Avenue entrance.

Charles A. Gill and noting as an aside that the well was finally shut down in 1962. With hardly a mention in the local papers that year, the medicinal waters of Gill Well that Dallas once thought would become a major health resort destination were capped.

Figure 9: Obadiah and Serena were buried at the Cochran Chapel Cemetery. The marker on the far left is Gabriel's, with smaller markers for three other family members. The church was the first in Dallas, built on land donated by Serena's sister, Nancy Jane Hughes Cochran, in 1844. The Dallas Weekly Herald eulogized Obadiah as "pure-minded and generous-hearted," and noted that he was "energetic and provident...had accumulated comfort and abundance." Such flowing praise for the deceased character and accomplishments was the normal journalistic style of the time. Photograph by Evelyn Montgomery.

partner Joe Ellett constructed not only a grist mill but a saw mill at this rare location where the flow of the river was easily harnessed. The Arlington Park Recreation Center was later built on the site. The sawmill meant farmers could improve their homes. Instead of building houses out of barely shaped tree trunks, they could buy standard building lumber and attractive exterior cladding for their homes. Such a house felt like progress, successful settlement, and respectability.

By the 1880s, the growing city needed to increase its clean water supply for the citizens. In 1887, the city purchased land along Turtle Creek and built a water processing facility. To supply it, they next bought the mill site at Record Crossing. Previous attempts to supply the city with water from the West Fork failed, as it carried Fort Worth's sewage and slaughterhouse waste. Water from the Elm Fork was much tastier. By 1896, the city had built a dam and pumping station at Record Crossing to send that good water through wooden pipes to the newly enlarged Turtle Creek Treatment Plant. That facility was just west of the later ballpark at Reverchon Park. Its 1909 pump station building was later used as the Sammons Center for the Arts. Two settling basins indented in the land were used to clear river mud from the water. The Record Crossing dam was no longer needed after 1930, supplanted by the Bachman dam and the lake it fed.

Record was a founding trustee of the Cochran Chapel Methodist Church, the first church in Dallas, established with a dedicated building in 1855. In 1861, he led the formation of a Home Guard, citizens prepared to protect the city from northern troops, which never became necessary. Members of the Record family intermarried with leading families of the northwest quadrant of Dallas: the Cochrans, Hughes, Knights, and Lemmons. Due to a surfeit of Record daughters instead of sons, the Record name does not live on in the social registry and political history quite as clearly as the names of his neighbors. George W. Record's legacy, or if you will allow, record, lives primarily in Record Crossing Road and Record Street downtown.

Several west Dallas pioneers other than John Record enjoy the honor of having current Dallasites remember their names through the streets of the city. Cole Avenue recalls Dr. Cole (whose name also graces a park,) and Knight Street intersects Harry Hines behind the World Trade Center. Five streets further toward the Medical District, Lucas Drive recalls Cedar Springs pioneer Alfred King Lucas. When the area left farming behind, Lucas subdivided his farm for new houses, between Lucas Drive and his other namesake street, Kings Road, to the north.

Kendall Street recalls the farm of the Kendall family, while Bradford Street was the later estate on Cedar Springs Road of T. Leonard Bradford, Jr. The Grigsby family's street is in old east Dallas rather than near the Medical District. As for Miles Bennett? Harry Hines began as a short rural road at the edge of his survey that was called Bennett Road. It was soon overshadowed by its other name, Grauwyler. John H. and Emma Grauwyler were Swiss immigrants to the Medical District. Widowed Emma bequeathed part of their farm to the city when

Figure 10: In this ambrotype dated about 1858, Serena Knight holds a baby, possibly one of her ten children, Epps Gabriel Knight. Courtesy of the DeGolyer Library, Southern Methodist University.

she died in 1923. It remains a city park, named in honor of her husband, at the northwest corner of the Medical District. And what of the thoroughfare that runs in front of the park. Does it recall Miles Bennett or John Grauwyler? Both pioneer names were abandoned in favor of the state highway commissioner who rebuilt it as an early highway, Harry Hines.

The honoring of important pioneers through street names continues. In 2008, the city changed the name of Motor Street (previously Amelia Street, of which little is left, previously Moxley Street) to Medical District Drive in recognition of the most recent pioneering force in the area. The growing wholesale marketing business in the area was recognized in 1984. The section of Industrial Avenue from Irving Boulevard to the "y" juncture with Harry Hines was renamed Market Center Boulevard. Members of the pioneer families surely hoped their lands would prosper in the future, but they could not have foreseen the course of development as the 1800s frontier moved into the 20th century city.

Figure 11: The new Record Crossing Dam was a vital work of infrastructure for the city. Apparently, it was also considered so attractive in its bucolic setting that it merited presentation on a postcard, to be sent to people in other cities so that they could see what was going on in Dallas. This one was mailed to San Diego, California in 1908. Courtesy of the Old Red Museum of Dallas County History and Culture.

Chapter 3

FROM RURAL OUTSKIRT TO PART OF THE CITY

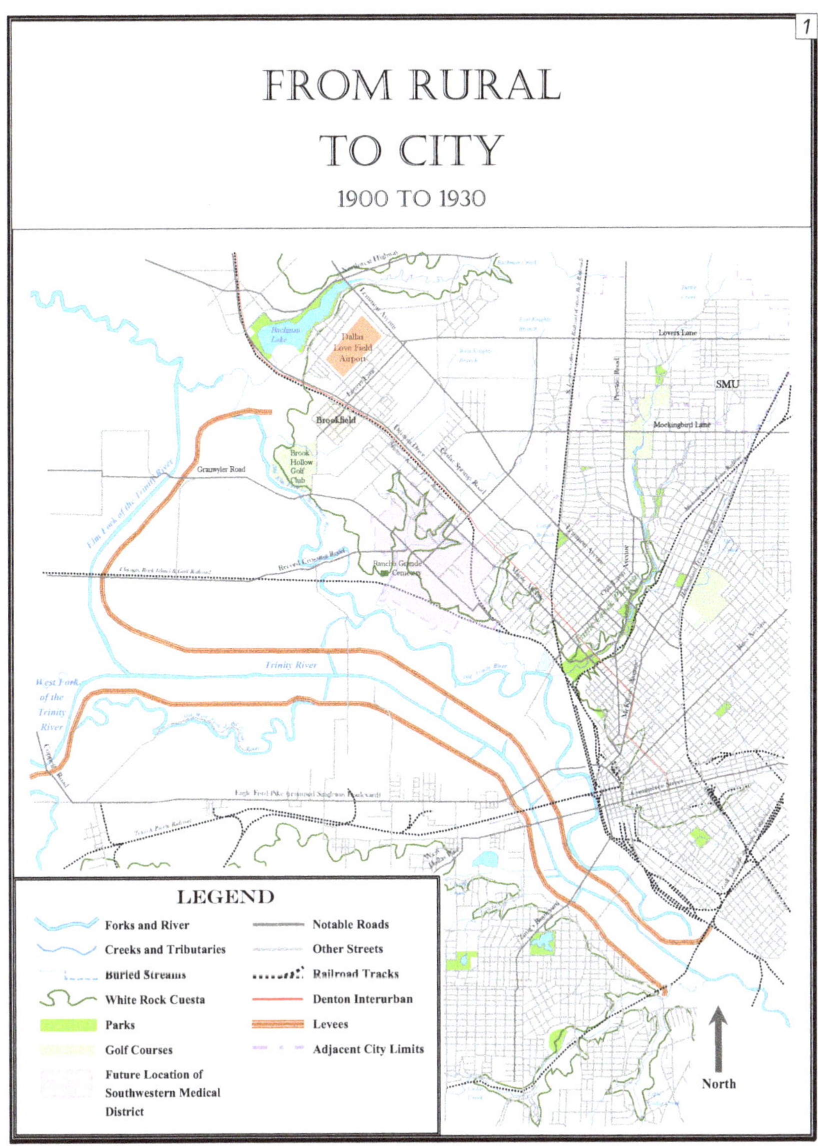

Figure 1: Key features of the developing Medical District area prior to World War II. Courtesy of Robert Prejean.

Figure 2: In 1937, the dotted line of the city limits followed a tortured, winding path that bypassed most Medical District lands to reach out and snag Love Field and some of the development near it. Image from "Latest Map of Dallas" sold by M. H. West, 1937. Courtesy of Old Red Museum of Dallas County History and Culture.

Any of the pioneer settlements could have become the urban center of the county—Cedar Springs, Dallas, Hord's Ridge, Letot, Garland, Wheatland, Lisbon. The crossing of two railroads in Dallas by 1873 ensured it would win the contest. John Neely Bryan's original site did indeed become the civic and commercial center of the county.

All lands and residents near the city could be considered part of the community of Dallas in people's minds. Legal incorporation into Dallas required annexation, to officially extend the city limits. This has never been a straightforward process.

Like all cities, Dallas has been most eager to annex lands when the benefits outweigh the costs. Benefits include growth of the tax base first and foremost, also increasing population, and potentially claiming beautiful or impressive sites. Costs involve the provision of city services to the annexed area, such as utilities, fire and police protection, trash service, and public schools. Before annexation, residents and businesses in an area depended on county government or provided these things for themselves but did not pay city taxes. Areas with industry and commerce were more profitable for the city to annex than residential. Very wealthy areas such as Highland Park and University

Park were desirable for annexation but resisted it because they did not want to take on Dallas' expensive obligations. The separate city of East Dallas was unwillingly annexed in 1889 to make Dallas the largest Texas city in the 1890 census.

Areas northwest of downtown, particularly the Medical District, were slow to be annexed, or really recognized as part of the city. Official efforts tended to follow events outside of the city's control that

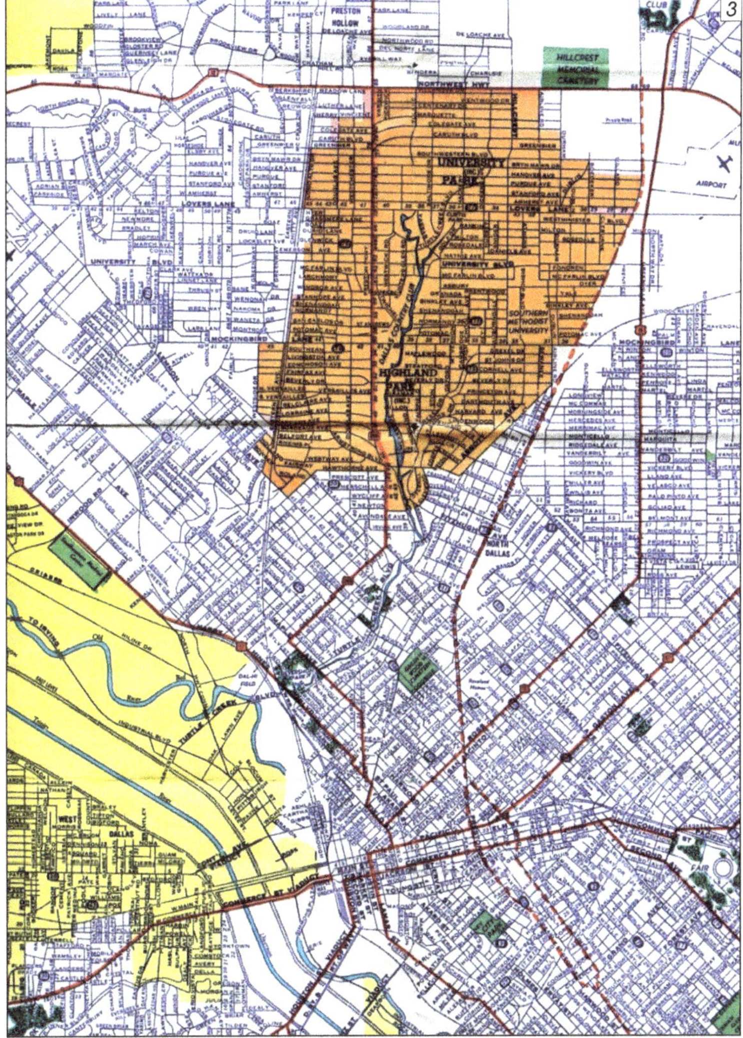

Figure 3: In 1949, all Medical District lands south of Harry Hines were outside the city limits, as indicated in yellow on the Ashburn's City Map of Dallas. Courtesy of Dallas-Fort Worth Freeways website.

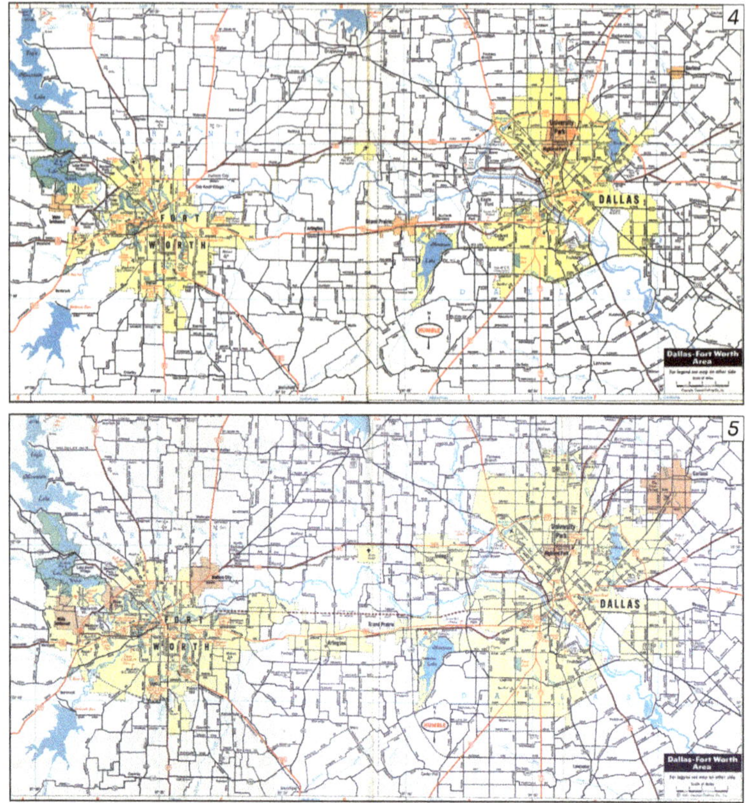

Figures 4 and 5: The 1954 Humble Dallas Fort Worth Area Map (above) shows that the city limits (in yellow) have not yet moved south of Harry Hines, though Parkland Hospital opened that year. In the 1956 version of the map (below), the lands for Parkland and the Southwestern Medical School have been annexed. Both are courtesy of the Dallas-Fort Worth Freeways website.

pulled the district slowly into the city, such as the creation and growth of Love Field, the birth of suburban neighborhoods in the area, and the westward expansion of hospital uses. The city expanded its limits to take in only what it wanted. The lands of the Medical District entered the city in a slow, piecemeal process lasting well into the 20th century.

RAILROADS

It is generally recognized that Dallas' opportunity to become a big city arrived with the rail lines: the Houston and Texas Central in 1872 and the Texas and Pacific in 1873. Becoming a railroad crossing made Dallas a shipping and manufacturing center. The population grew and so did opportunities for profit.

Those first two lines missed the Medical District, but Dallas became a rail center and later lines carefully threaded their way along the cuesta and the Elm Fork. In 1874, the Dallas and Wichita Falls was built. Later named the Missouri, Kansas, and Texas, or KATY, its path started downtown and skirted the cuesta on the southern side before going to Farmers Branch. The last line to enter Dallas during the early railroad boom was the Chicago, Rock Island and Pacific, in 1903. It came up from Houston and continued on to Fort Worth, passing through downtown and squeezing between the KATY and the Elm Fork.

Railroad tracks did not really help rural residents go to town to shop or do business. For early routine transportation, horses and wagons traversed wagon roads. These dirt roads usually followed the boundaries of land parcels and naturally connected the most common destinations. Since their routes logically responded to local needs and they lay at the edge of private property, they were easily converted into permanent roads as settlement increased. In a familiar pattern, the main northwesterly wagon trail of the 1860s, from downtown Dallas to Farmers Branch, went by way of Cedar Springs, avoiding both the cuesta and the Medical District. It was generally the route of Lemmon Avenue, which continued to guide local development. Smaller wagon roads within the District did eventually develop into modern roadways, including Harry Hines.

Sam Street's Map of Dallas County includes both these early wagon roads and the locations of houses in 1900. Those two types of early rural development naturally followed each other, and neither is evenly spread through the county. A wide swath moving northwest from downtown along the Elm Fork is sparsely populated with little squares for owner occupied houses and triangles for

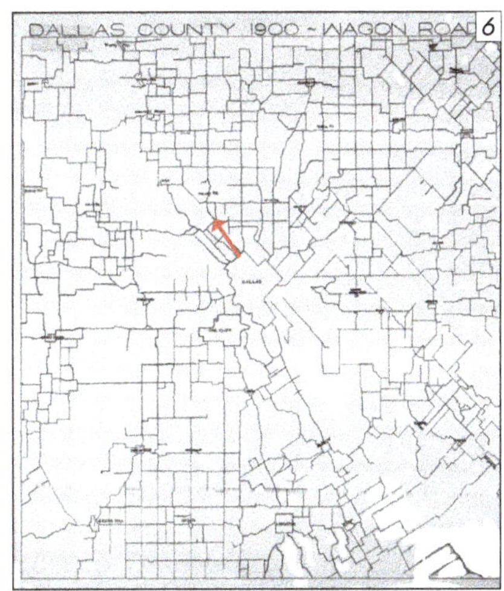

Figure 6: This map by M.C. Toyer isolates the wagon roads on shown on Sam Street's 1900 map of Dallas County. The arrow indicates the one that traces the route of Lemmon Avenue. Courtesy of Dallas Public Library.

Figures 7 and 8: Sam Street's full map shows concentrations of triangles and squares in other areas of Dallas County. These symbols for houses are far fewer in the Medical District area, roughly the area around and below the red number 19. The second image is a close-up of the Medical District's few homes, one of which is identified as a store. Courtesy of Dallas County, Texas, Dallas Public Library, Dallas History and Archives, M17.

tenanted ones. Elsewhere in the county, smaller pockets of similarly sparse houses exist, most along the south side of the West Fork or the southeastern reaches of the main Trinity River. The little symbols for houses in the natural process of urban growth did not appear to be leading the Medical District to dense settlement or commercial use.

By 1900 Dallas had reason to dream of becoming an important city. It had established itself as a major transportation and wholesale trade center in the Southwest. It then gained recognition as an important city for banking, insurance, and the retail businesses. Leading families grew wealthier, and their sons and daughters traveled the nation and the world. Even the more modestly successful could ride a train to see a World's Fair in Chicago in 1893 or St. Louis in 1904. Everybody came home with ideas that could make Dallas more beautiful and a better place to live. City leaders were called upon to do something.

In 1911, they entered into the business of formal planning for city growth, by hiring planning expert George Kessler. His beautifully illustrated report, "A City Plan for Dallas," guided city efforts in the following years, even if the city failed to follow it completely. Kessler favored urban beauty through parks and beautiful streets and recognized the negative developmental effects of railroads.[1] Perhaps responding to established attractive residential areas, his proposed system of parks and boulevards excluded the Medical District and the southeastern part of the city, favoring Oak Cliff, the Park Cities, and the areas of the former city of East Dallas. The closest suggested improvement to the Medical District was the Turtle Creek Parkway, to ensure a pleasant journey from downtown to Highland Park. Only a few of his suggestions was completely carried out, but many city officials lived near the route of this beautification effort.

EARLY INSTITUTIONS IN THE AREA OF THE DISTRICT

Open land and sparse habitation are attractive for some uses. The northwest edge of the Medical District was chosen by the Army's Signal Corps for an aviation training camp in preparation for World War I. The Dallas Chamber of Commerce leased the land to the Army. Construction was almost complete in 1917 when the facility was

---

1   On Kessler's planning principals, see Wilson, William H, *The City Beautiful Movement*, Baltimore: Johns Hopkins University Press, 1989. In addition to this overall study, Wilson also wrote "Adapting to Growth: Dallas, Texas, and the Kessler Plan, 1908-1933," *Arizona and the West*, 25, 3 (Autumn 1983) pp. 245-260.

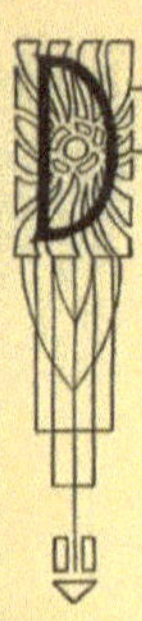  

A CITY PLAN FOR DALLAS

A. INNER SYSTEM

1. Boulevards and Parkways for Dallas

1. TURTLE CREEK PARKWAY

This parkway follows in a general way the windings of the creek. It is proposed to construct on each side of the stream a 40 foot driveway with accompanying sidewalk and grass spots, which will serve to connect adjoining

FOREST PARK

park areas. The parkway will commence at about Lake Avenue and extend northerly to Highland Park Addition, which in itself contains a beautiful parkway and is a natural continuation of the Turtle Creek improvement. This proposed development will enhance the present scenic value of Turtle Creek, and will become one of the most important links in the boulevard system. In addition, however, it will be the direct means of conserving the high class character of an important residential section and of furnishing it with a direct and convenient thoroughfare to the heart of the city.

Page Thirty-one

Figure 9: Kessler's plan for the boulevards and parkways of Dallas placed them in the areas of higher population, completely missing the Medical District lands between Maple Avenue and the Elm Fork. Courtesy of the Dallas Public Library.

Figure 10: Love Field Aviation Flying School, photographer credited as Johnson, 1918, 2003 Miscellany Collection, Dallas Public Library, Dallas History and Archives.

Figure 11: Cars Approaching Love Field for "Flyin' Frolic," photograph from an album, creator and date unknown, Dallas Municipal Archives, DSMA_01003_00125. May be viewed on The Portal to Texas History at ark:/67531/metapth66619. Figure 12: General view, "Flyin' Frolic," Nov. 12-13, 19118, Love Field, Tex., creator unknown, 1918, City Photographers Collection, Dallas Public Library, Dallas History and Archives, PA87-1/19-59-204.

named for Lieutenant Moss L. Love, who had recently been killed in a training exercise in San Diego. His death while practicing to become a pilot illustrates why the airfield was located far from the city center. Such potential accidents were less dangerous to the public in a sparsely populated area.

Pilots in training arrived at the end of 1917. A total of 449 of them were trained at Love Field. Those young men and their planes were of great interest to the people of Dallas. Local men were encouraged to enlist, and they were able to form their own unit. The distance to Love Field was not enough to stop people from coming out and watching the aerial maneuvers, though military security tried to keep them away, lest they discover military secrets. Dallasites enjoyed supporting the trainees. They invited them to meals and concerts, knitted them sweaters, and donated record albums for their listening pleasure.

After the war, the field was deactivated and the land and improvements reverted to the chamber of commerce. They initially used it for civilian pilot training and to bring in airmail. The chamber established the Love Field Improvement District to make the most of the facility for the benefit of local commerce. By 1924, the airfield and its attendant industries required enough labor that the Brookfield Addition was created to the southwest to provide housing.[2] This was not a sign the area was becoming a part of the city, quite the opposite. This was a solution to the problem of retaining labor in a place so far from settled residential areas. It was like an outpost of settlement.

The houses were typical small designs of the 1920s, sometimes called "American Basic", often with a total of four rooms plus bathroom and minimal exterior decoration. They were offered at prices and lending terms geared to the needs of the target buyers.[3] Gravel streets with curbs and gutter, as well as the luxury of full utility services, attracted buyers. The proximity of jobs and public transportation service via the Denton Interurban streetcar line was also enticing. Maple Avenue or Grauwyler offered easy automobile access downtown, but individual car ownership was not as common in 1924 among the working class.

In 1927, the city of Dallas bought Love Field. Its use had vastly expanded. Famous pilots and new types of planes visited. Local amateur pilots used Love Field. Special events like national conferences chartered planes to deliver attendees in style. The city wanted a municipal airport to serve citizens, and because that was the new mark of a great city. They began to build conveniences for casual air passengers as general air travel was poised to become a regular part of American life. Surely this change would have to draw Love Field, and the northwest in general, closer to the city at last.

The only other destination near Love Field was the Brook Hollow Golf Club, which opened in 1921. The story of its creation is quite a good one, worth telling even if it cannot really be proven. In 1921,

<hr>

2 "Addition will be Named Brookfield," *The Dallas Morning News*, Sept. 7, 1924, p. 1.
3 "Brookfield Suburb Homes Being Built," *The Dallas Morning News*, Feb. 1, 1925, p. 1.

Figures 13 and 14: Grounds and original small clubhouse at the Brook Hollow Golf Club in 1925. Artwork of Dallas 1925 Collection, Dallas Public Library, Dallas History and Archives.

Dallas businessman Cameron Buxton was outraged while playing at the Lakewood Country Club. His shot was ruined when his ball sank into a soft pile of worm castings. He determined that annoying worms were an intrinsic feature of a course built on the black clay that dominated in most of Dallas, along with terrible mud and cracked soil in dry weather.[4]

Whether or not it was the worms that led him and other golfers to seek better soil for golfing, they succeeded in finding a suitable site. They purchased a piece of farmland with sandy soil that would discourage worms and other problems associated with the soil of the black land prairie. It was also close to the Elm Fork for irrigating the grass, and the land had gentle hills. The soil was described as "sandy and sandy loam underlain by clay and gravel." That was thought perfect

---

4   The story was included by Frances James in her "History of Golf in Dallas," written in 1999 for the Dallas County Pioneer Association and available on their website, https://dallaspioneer.org.

for Bermuda grass and is the type of less-rich soil associated with the typical Cross Timbers tree varieties like Post Oak. The 1924 Soil Map and Soil Survey of Dallas County from the U.S. Department of Agriculture confirms that the soil was identified as Cahaba Fine Sandy Soil, not widespread in Dallas County and mostly found outside the Trinity Clay areas that line the river. So, the club's soil assessment was correct.

The location was six miles away from downtown on Grauwyler Road, the future Harry Hines Boulevard. It may have been purchased from George A. Holland, who owned a country home in the area named Brook Hollow.[5] In 1919, when he hosted a wedding, it was described as being on Maple Avenue Road, as was the golf course. The Brook Hollow name is attributed to a brook on the course that flowed into a hollow.

The club hired nationally renowned golf course designer A. W. Tillinghast to plan a championship course. His design maximized the natural features of the land and the course became a regular location for important golfing events. They hosted local and regional tournaments and their players often won against those of other local clubs, and even visiting professionals. The club continued to grow and prosper as the developing medical facilities and other urban uses crept around it.

Another institution attracted by the Elm Fork was Trinity Farm. This commercial agricultural enterprise took advantage of the rich soil in the bottomlands. Trinity Farm was a large venture that grew food for Dallasites and for rail shipment to other Texas locations. The produce included fruits and pecans. The farm's eight square miles of land lay mostly to the west of the Elm Fork, but it included land on the east side at Record Crossing.

It was owned by outside investors from Tulsa, Wichita Falls, and Waxahachie. Unlike nearby family farms, where the owner might work by the side of hired help, this was a corporate operation of absentee owners, hired managers, and laborers. The company mostly employed recent immigrants from Mexico and African Americans. They were provided with on-site housing, segregated schools, and a store for necessities. It was essentially a company town, five miles from downtown Dallas with no easy transport. Such towns provided for the needs

---

5   Mr. and Mrs. Holland hosted a wedding in their home in 1919, mentioned in "Dallas Social
     Affairs," *The Dallas Morning News*, Nov. 10, 1919, p. 7.

Figure 15: Jesús Hernández worked for Trinity Farms. He poses here with his family at their home there, date unknown. Courtesy of Dallas Mexican American Historical League.

Figure 16: Only a small snapshot is available of this event in the cemetery, date unknown. White crosses marking each grave and people are gathered near the gazebo. Courtesy of the Dallas Mexican American Historical League.

of workers, but also maintained a great deal of control over them. The company was the employer, landlord, and retail provider all in one, giving the workers little freedom to challenge working conditions or prices at the store. The farm lasted until the 1930s, when the rerouting of the river opened the land above the Elm Fork to industrial development, which displaced agricultural uses.

One amenity the company provided remains, the Rancho Grande Cemetery. This burial ground for employees is south of Record Crossing Road near Harry Hines. Forty-one graves have been located, though not all of the deceased's names and circumstances are known. Francis James, Dallas' legendary cemetery expert, thought there might be about fifty.[6] The graves are racially segregated, as would be expected for the era. The earliest documented burial was 1919, only two years after investors assembled the land. General use of the cemetery probably ended in 1945, with the last burial in 1954.

PIONEER FAMILIES BUILDING THE CITY

Descendants of the northwestern pioneers headed downtown to become Dallas leaders as the city matured. The early landowners there tended to intermarry and to intermingle their land and other business deals. Along with the Knight family, these included the Lemmon, Cole, Hughes, Harris and Cochran families. Some generations contained many children. Obadiah Knight fathered seventeen children; his brother Gabriel had nineteen.

Two of Obadiah's sons represent the next stage of prosperity and civic leadership attainable by the second generation of pioneers. His oldest son, Epps, took the family love of land in a new direction. As an early real estate agent, he was quite a force in pulling former farmland into use for the expanding city. He was born on the farm in 1858, and, with his brothers and sisters, grew up doing chores. His intermittent boyhood education, including attendance at the Cedar Springs Academy on his father's original land, culminated at the E. B. Lawrence Commercial College downtown. Such commercial colleges prepared men to engage in business.

He married a local girl, Miss Fanny Patton, whose childhood home stood on the site of the Majestic Theater.[7] They built a house in 1889, renowned as a mansion, on Cedar Springs Road near Oak Lawn. It was three stories tall with stylish Queen Anne decoration. Given his family

---

6   Frances James' discussed both the cemetery and the whole of Trinity Farms in her book *Dallas County History—From the Ground Up*, (no publisher, 2007), pp. 35-6. For a fuller examination of the subject, including a list of known burials in the cemetery, see Ed Mills, "Trinity Farm and El Rancho Grande Cemetery Burials," *The Dallas Journal*, vol. 50, 2004, pp. 3-33.

7   "Epps G. Knight, 85, Dallas Pioneer, Dies," *The Dallas Morning News*, Nov. 8, 1943, p. 1.

Figures 17 and 18: R.E.L. Knight and his house on Maple Avenue, demolished in 1942. Courtesy of Thompson Knight LLC and the Dallas Public Library.

tradition of large families, Epps included seven bedrooms though he and Fanny went on to produce only nine children.

That year, he really began leaving the management of the family farm behind, in favor of real estate, with his own firm. He was elected to the first of three terms as county tax collector in 1896. In 1919, he began two years as an oil man in Wichita Falls and became quite rich. He supported local organizations and served on company boards. He outlived all of his siblings, dying in his home at the age of eighty-five. His heirs sold the house for the construction of an office building.[8] Their entrepreneurial father, who loved to try new businesses, probably would have approved.

Another successful son was Robert E. Lee Knight, who usually used his initials. R.E.L. went further afield for his education than his brother. He graduated from Southwestern University in Georgetown in 1886 and earned his law degree at the University of Texas. Having thus transformed some of his father's farming wealth into professional accreditation, he left behind all things agricultural. The business of law was still young in Dallas. It centered on the new red courthouse built in 1892 and now called Old Red. The small legal community gathered their offices around the courthouse square, where most of Dallas' retail establishments were also located. R.E.L. was a founding partner in one

---

8   The demolition of the house at 3617 Cedar Springs Road was recorded in "Old Knight Place Being Torn Down," *The Dallas Morning News*, May 5, 1957, p. 16.

of the earliest firms in the city, Finley, Knight & Harris. It grew to become Thompson, Knight, Baker and Harris and endure as a Dallas institution.

"Colonel Bob," as R.E.L. was sometimes called, also worked in local and state politics and for the Democratic Party. Friends with governors and judges, he served for years as the director of the State Fair. He belonged to all of the important local clubs and clearly knew how to build, and use, his connections. He died of a heart attack in his own home on Maple Avenue in 1936. He and his brother Epps led opposing local groups on the issue of prohibition. Epps was for it; R. E. L. was for liquor.

An elementary school was named for Obadiah when it opened in 1930. It is located north of the Medical District, near Love Field. Epps spoke of his father's pioneer adventures at the opening ceremony. His folksy stories painted Obadiah as a feisty fighter and a Texas maverick. *The Dallas Morning News* produced a cartoon to accompany the story on Epps' speech. It depicts Obadiah as a cantankerous, hardy pioneer, his horse stuck in the river as he tries to reach Dallas to vote for Cedar Springs to be the county seat. Though Obadiah's sons had moved far from their father's world, they seemed to revere his pioneer spirit and to continue it as they helped build a city.

THE TRINITY RIVER AND NEW INDUSTRIAL PLANNING

Flooding was an ongoing threat to downtown Dallas. By the early 20th century, the city was ready to invest a fortune to keep the waters at bay. The flood of 1908 was particularly bad. It washed out bridges, leaving Oak Cliff cut off from downtown. The public and commercial buildings of courthouse square were flooded, impacting commerce and government operations. Five people were killed and 4,000 left homeless.

The levee-building project would not begin for twenty years, in 1928. Five years of labor was needed to move 22 million cubic yards of dirt to redirect the channels and build the levees. It was completed in 1933. John Neely Bryan wouldn't have recognized his beloved river. It was moved away from downtown, its curling course straightened. The most serious relocation occurred near the District, where the confluence of the main river, the Elm Fork, and the West Fork was dramatically changed. The Elm Fork moved to the south. Its former

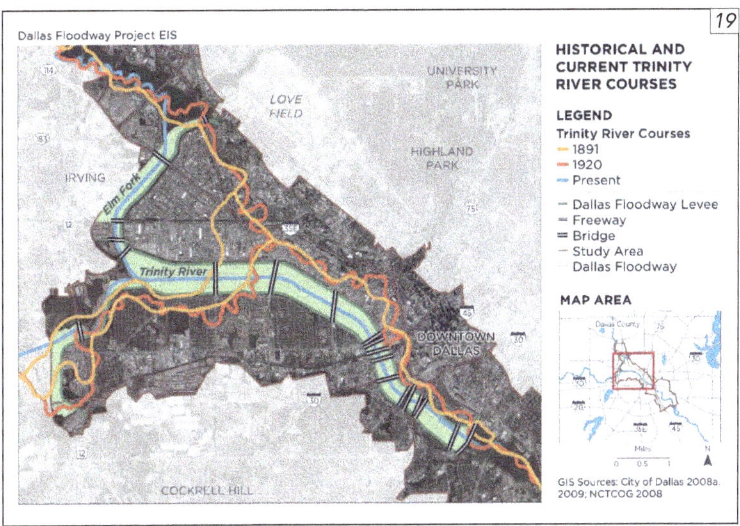

Figure 19: This map depicts the original course of the river and its course with the levee system. Courtesy of Troy Oxford.

Figure 20: In this aerial image, the levee system is seen cutting across the lower left corner, and the original serpentine river route is visible above. The trapezoidal shape in the upper right is the water reservoir for the Turtle Creek Treatment Plant, from 1896. That shape would later define the site of Cobb Stadium. Courtesy of the Foscue Map Library, Southern Methodist University.

Figure 21: A model of the future industrial center was displayed at the State Fair, with airplanes flying overhead. Courtesy of The Dallas Morning News.

Figure 22: In this 1956 image we see many industrial buildings fill the space between the old and new channels of the Trinity River, as intended. The older, serpentine channel was still a deep and tree-lined feature on the landscape. Photograph from "Pictures Tell Story of Trinity Industrial District," The Dallas Morning News, published October 18, 1930. Copyright [1930] The Dallas Morning News, Inc.

course became more buildable land available near the Medical District. The proper use for that land was initially unclear. Those who might consider building there feared that the danger of flooding had not been eliminated, it had just moved further away.[9]

George Kessler, the city planner who originally recommended the river relocation, had a suggestion. He wrote "low lands outside and adjacent to these levees would provide additional room for railroad terminals and switching properties." The area was isolated, branded as unsafe and as undesirable for residential and business use. In 1930, the city concurred. They paved a street in the new lands created by the levee and named it Industrial Boulevard. The surrounding lands were designated the Trinity Industrial District, planned for new manufacturers who would increase Dallas' production and jobs base. Development along Industrial Blvd. was slow during the 1930s. The Great Depression was not a good time for business expansion or new construction. Floods in 1938 and 1941 proved that the levees were capable of protecting the new industrial district, reassuring potential investors just as the Depression yielded to war preparations. The city finally saw good sales of land along Industrial in 1946. Buyers included the Texas and Pacific Railroad, which built a new freight center. At the exact same time, the earliest medical institutions of the future Medical District were being planned. How the two would live side by side was yet to be determined.

---

9   Robert B. Fairbanks explains the complex negotiations among Dallas leaders that made the levees possible in "The Great Divide: The Politics of Space and the First Trinity River Valley Controversy," in *Legacies: A History Journal for Dallas and North Central Texas*, 27, 1, Spring, 2015, pp. 48–60. He also documented how citizen organizations argued for and against the plan in "Making Better Citizens in Dallas: The Kessler Plan Association and Consensus Building in the 1920s," *Legacies: A History Journal for Dallas and North Central Texas*, 11, 2, Fall, 1999, pp. 26–38.

HARRY HINES
AND HIS HIGHWAY

In its history, Dallas has hosted two frequent visitors named Harry Hines. The first one entertained here in the 1920s, but "eccentric Harry Hines," the "nut comic," did not build the city a highway and grace it with his name.[1] That honor was reserved for Harry Hines the Texas State Highway Commissioner. His local speaking engagements during the 1930s and 1940s were almost as popular as a comic act, when he told various civic groups about the exciting promise of new highways reaching Dallas.

Figure 1: Commissioner Harry Hines spoke at the opening celebration for the Triple Underpass in 1936. The underpass was created to be part of the Centennial ceremonial route to Fair Park. Image courtesy of Dallas Morning News Collection, DeGolyer Library, Southern Methodist University.

In 1925, Hines was only thirty-eight years old when his Wichita Falls company, Knight and Hines, sold $2 million worth of oil land in the Panhandle. He became not only a leader in the oil industry but in the promotion of evangelical Christianity throughout the state. He was an organizer of a national conference in Fort Worth in 1929 titled "Evangelism by Laymen" and was the founder of the Texas Layman's League of Christian Churches. This work continued until his death in 1954.

He was also interested in the improvement of transportation, particularly highways, which would benefit both the oil industry and the growing number of automobile owners who wanted to travel for fun.

---

1   Also known as "Happy Harry Hines," the vaudevillian was both a singer and comic and played at the Majestic Theater, as reported in "A Bachelor Dinner," in *The Dallas Morning News*, Oct. 24, 1915, p. 4.

Figure 2: Harry Hines is second from the left in this image of State Highway Department officials enjoying a barbeque in 1937. One of the purposes of the new highways was to give Texans access to recreational facilities like this one, Swift's Camp. Image courtesy of the University of Texas at Arlington. Originally appeared in the Fort Worth Star-Telegram.

Such travelers in the early decades of the 20th century often found few usable roads between cities. In 1917, the federal government created a program to fund highway construction, and the state created the Texas Highway Department (now the Texas Department of Transportation) to oversee planning and construction.

Because of his interest in highways, in 1936 Hines was appointed to the chairmanship of the Texas State Highway Commission, the group that oversaw the Highway Department. He promoted highway beautification through landscaping, and roadside rest and recreational areas for leisure "autoists," as drivers were sometimes called. He himself traveled roadways extensively to speak at all sorts of events across the region. In Dallas, he spoke to the Chamber of Commerce, churches, civic organizations, and women's groups. He was loved throughout North Central Texas because he ensured the region received a significant share of those highways. He secured state funds for improvements near Dallas in preparation for the 1936 Centennial exposition.

In a 1933 plan for the Dallas highway system, the road that would become Harry Hines was called the Northwest Connection. It started Dallas travelers on their way to Denton and Wichita Falls and served as a northerly route to Fort Worth. The new road was a speedy improvement over the previous path along Maple Avenue. Local media were impressed with the four concrete lanes and median in the middle.

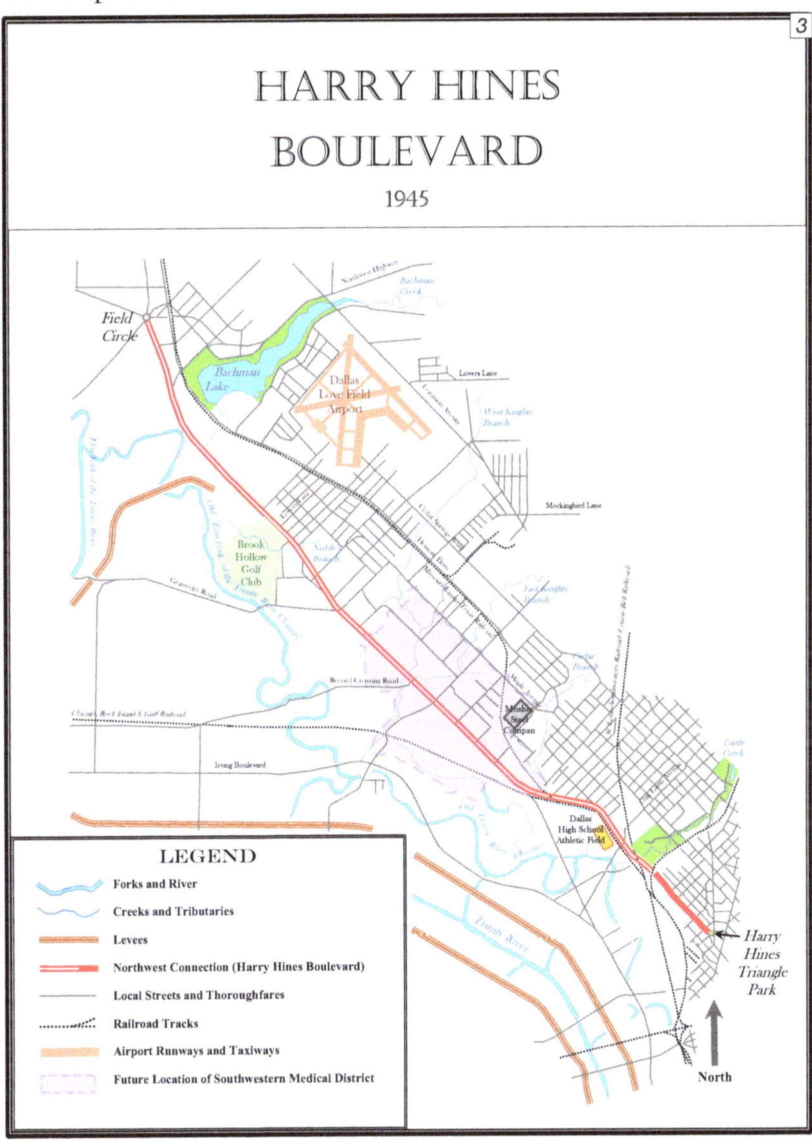

Figure 3: Map of the key features of the Medical District area when Harry Hines Boulevard was new. Courtesy of Robert Prejean.

It was viewed as a wonderful entrance into Dallas, and, at the time of its opening, termed a "super highway." By 1941, the highway was nearing completion, and many people moved to name it for Harry Hines, though the name was not made official by the Dallas City Council until 1948. He was honored at the dedication in October of that year, where highway promoters spoke of the need to continue funding and building such wonderful roads.

Though highways were fairly new, they were already known to cause two changes to lands along their routes: rising property values and unsightly landscapes full of billboards. Landowners along the Harry Hines' route were not sure exactly what type of buyers to seek in 1941. They advertised acreage for sale as suitable for county home sites, mass subdivisions, or industrial and commercial uses.

The State of Texas was calling on local citizens to support a cause dear to both Mr. Hines and Eleanor Roosevelt, the beautification of highways. In Dallas, groups engaged in landscaping, including wildflowers, and encouraged landowners along the route to volunteer to help. The goal was to avoid a shabby, rundown look. Locals were so proud of the new highway that a painting of it by Ramon Froman was included in the 1947 exhibit by the Federation of Dallas Artists.

Figure 4: Traffic maneuvering along the new Harry Hines Boulevard at Record Crossing Road. This photograph was taken to record traffic conditions. Courtesy of the Dallas Public Library.

The new highway did bring increasing development to the area. Some of that development was oriented to tourists. Automobile drivers needed gas stations. This new institution was still evolving in the 1940s. The early ones were often located at the site of a large oil company facility. In naming their small business, many owners used both a unique identifier and their national corporate affiliation. Both of these were true of Chet's Sinclair Service Station which opened in 1955 at 5200 Harry Hines. Chet was Chester J. Fiorello, who lived in the Medical District on Brown Street. His station was conveniently located in front of a Sinclair refining and distribution center. Sinclair service stations are few in number today but were once a common sight. The Kansas-based company grew rapidly during and after World War II. Chet's sign may have featured their cheerful mascot, Dino the Dinosaur. He had the long neck of a brontosaurus and looked proud of the role he played in providing people with oil.

Figure 5: Visitors to the Texas Centennial in 1936 saw a replica of Dino the Dinosaur at the Sinclair company exhibit. Courtesy of Mary Newton Maxwell.

Tourists also needed overnight accommodations. Highway-oriented alternatives to downtown hotels developed their own building forms beginning in the 1930s. One popular option was a group of separate cabins, offering economy and a feeling of privacy to the increasing number of families taking automobile vacations. Tourists also appreciated fun, thematic architecture, and a matching name. Seventy-Seven Ranch Tourist Court at Harry Hines and Lucas was a curved line of attached units called cabins, each with its own entrance, porch, and parking, surrounding a courtyard. The name referenced its location on highway 77, the state name for Harry Hines Blvd. outside of Dallas. Its sign was in the shape of a saguaro cactus. The brick building with a red roof resembled a very long ranch house. The interiors were wood-

Figure 6: Postcard for the 77 Ranch Tourist Court. On the reverse side, it reads "Truly one of the finest Courts of Texas. Three minutes from downtown." Courtesy of Evelyn Montgomery.

paneled. Other nearby motels in 1951 were the Trav-O-Tel at Hondo Avenue and the Dal-Hi Motor Court at Vegas Street.

Both tourists and locals needed food. The Four Brothers Café near Butler Street offered meals and fresh eggs from the family farm in Grapevine, only fifty-five cents a dozen. Hammons Drive-In Restaurant occupied the southwest corner of Harry Hines and Inwood. In 1947, that location was offered for sale, a drive-in café with liquor license. High future profits were certain because a $9,000,000 construction project was underway right next door—the Southwestern Medical School, with students who would presumably be hungry and thirsty.

Over the years, the very name of Harry Hines took on an association with the darker side of life. Vices such as gambling and prostitution were always most prevalent at the edges of the city, with open space, few concerned neighbors, and less notice from law enforcement. Harry Hines Boulevard itself may have contributed by offering easy access for customers and egress in the event that the law arrived.

Gambling was a significant concern during the early years of the boulevard, particularly in the 1950s. Along with selling fresh eggs and quick meals, Richard and John Piano of the Four Brothers Café saw potential profit in hosting gaming. They were the first Dallasites to apply for a new 1951 federal tax stamp to allow them to operate legal gambling.

A few blocks further west, a nightclub called the Crazy Castle was much more active and much less legal in their gambling operation. Owner Paul Wyche and his tenant Lawrence Burch were two of five men charged in March 1951 with running an illegal gambling operation at this location. Gambling included a slot machine and "sudden death crap games," which the house always won. Trouble with the law continued. By 1960, the location was operated as The Southerner, a night club with live music. The proprietor, twenty-four-year-old Mrs. Merril Ann Warren, almost lost her license to serve beer because of frequent infractions of the law cited by Dallas police.

A 1951 raid of a gambling den at 5500 Harry Hines revealed professional gamblers fleecing customers in rigged games. Vice squad detectives described the security setup of the nightclub. It included a small entry chamber with one-way glass and a peephole, so that staff could identify potential patrons before granting admittance. Even the otherwise legitimate and socially restricted Brook Hollow Country Club was raided in 1961. The 200 gamblers were mostly betting on horse races. The seven men operating the event included staff members of the club.

Prostitution was a continuing scourge in early Dallas, and later followed the new highway out from downtown. The city of Dallas briefly designated an official location for prostitution in 1910. Frogtown

Figure 7: The Dal-Hi Motor Courts was located at 4300 Harry Hines. Its colorful appearance belied the shady goings-on within. The owner was cited in 1956 for allowing prostitutes to operate out of his facility. Courtesy of the Boston Public Library.

was located northwest of Pacific Avenue near the current West End, in a blighted neighborhood. Prostitution was legalized in that area in the hope that it would be contained and that respectable citizens, particularly ladies, would never have to see evidence of its existence. The experiment lasted three years. Left to its natural course, areas of prostitution naturally drift toward parts of the city where the trade meets the least resistance. This could describe parts of Harry Hines and even of the Medical District in the mid-20th century.

In 1956, Clarence Green was charged with operating a "bawdy house" at the Dal-Hi Motor Courts. The warrant for his arrest followed eighty individual arrests of prostitutes at his motel. By 1979, little had changed but the language used to describe such hotel practices. The Park Crest Hotel at 4318 Harry Hines, at Arroyo, was called a "hooker haven." This implied a rather looser relationship to the prostitutes who made use of its hourly rental rates but spent more time outside, luring customers. In the 1970s and 1980s, rising property values and development of medical uses and other legitimate businesses pushed the red light district further up Harry Hines. The common image became that of the provocatively dressed prostitute walking the boulevard, appealing to potential customers.

That era also saw barely veiled sexually-oriented businesses, such as massage parlors and nude modeling studios. Both promoted prostitution. The nude modeling studios were legal and unregulated until City Council member Ricardo Medrano proposed a new ordinance in 1982.

Figure 8: The El Azteca Café moved to Harry Hines at Inwood in 1955. They advertised "specializing in typical Mexican Dishes—reasonably priced." Courtesy of the Dallas Public Library.

CHAPTER 4

Figure 9: In the mid-fifties, signs along Harry Hines warned drivers to slow down, not drink, and get a driver's license. Courtesy of the Dallas Public Library.

Figure 10: In June of 1951, Mack E. Mahoney of Lancaster collided with a metal light pole at Harry Hines and Amelia Street. He suffered minor injuries. Courtesy of the Dallas Public Library.

Throughout its early years, Harry Hines was also known for automobile accidents. In 1955, *The Dallas Morning News* city editor Jack B. Kreuger wrote: "The ride along Harry Hines, assuming you come through Field Circle in one piece, is always a thrill, of course. Here the trucks run, like fish, in schools and the driving is tricky." The nature of the street, a divided boulevard of multiple lanes, may have encouraged recklessness. City officials proclaimed it a "high-accident" street in

1948, when a large increase in accidents was noted. Police said that many speeders they cited were "the best people and not criminals" but that they needed to learn to drive. By the 1950s, Dallas was slowly installing traffic signals in the city to help such hapless drivers. Such installations were quite newsworthy because they were new, a response to the sudden increase in driving. The first one on Harry Hines was at Industrial in 1950, the second at Amelia in 1951.

The presence of water features also posed dangers. Remnants of the relocated river and the buried creeks attracted swimmers. In 1954, Colin Strickland drowned in the old river bed near Record Crossing while his wife watched helplessly. A year earlier, a sixteen-year-old boy from Arlington Park also drowned in that abandoned river channel. Three people plunged into the flood-swollen Bachman Creek in 1947, when the Denton Drive Bridge collapsed. Mrs. Lois Marman was carried downstream to Harry Hines, where she grabbed a floating log until police rescued her.

And finally, Harry Hines was plagued with equines running wild among the populous, and one errant toddler on a tricycle. The gradual

A young adventurer and his slightly frightened mother. . . . Michael Everett, two, and new to tricycle riding, seems not at all ruffled after braving the traffic of Harry Hines Boulevard Thursday morning. His mother, though, hopes it won't happen again.

RIDES BOULEVARD STRIPE

2-Year-Old Tricyclist Starts on World Tour

Two-year-old Michael Everett grew tired of his back yard at 2311 Vagas Thursday morning. Busy Harry Hines Boulevard, one block away, seemed to offer a perfect avenue to his unexplored world.

Young Mike, without the caution acquired from experience, mounted his tricycle—which he learned to ride three weeks ago—and rode away. The boulevard was his first stop.

Innocent of traffic laws, Mike could scarcely be expected to know which lane of the boulevard was reserved for tricycle traffic.

He selected the black stripe separating the two lanes on the east side of the boulevard and started toward town. The heavy flow of early morning traffic parted as respectfully as the Red Sea of Bible times.

Finally a motorist, Dalton F. Evans of 1245 Bishop, stopped and picked up the child and his tricycle and took them to the safety of the curb.

Mrs. Gerald C. Everett, his mother, meanwhile had missed young Mike. She saw Evans parked at the curb, went to investigate and found her son.

"I was so scared I couldn't punish him," she later said, "but I'll bet he doesn't get out of the back yard again soon. I bought a length of new rope, and it'll take a magician to untie the knots I put on the gate."

Figure 11: Mike Everett and his frightened mother posed for a newspaper photographer. Courtesy of The Dallas Morning News.

transition of the Medical District from a rural to an urban nature was the source of the equine issues, though that does not explain why they were all the same color. In 1946, a sorrel horse was reported to have strayed at Harry Hines and Inwood. One year later, a red sorrel horse was lost near 5710 Harry Hines. Hopefully both were found. A 1948 advertisement suggests a potential source. Prewitt Stables, 5912 Harry Hines, advertised a registered Tennessee walking horse, sorrel in color, named Wilson's Successor. He was probably not related to the next escapee, a sorrel mule named Francis. In 1953, Francis led Park Patrolman D. C. Betts, Sr. in a chase down Harry Hines. She was taken to the animal shelter and not immediately claimed.

In 1948, Michael Everett became an impassioned proponent of cycling on city streets. Unfortunately, he was only two years old when he headed toward downtown on his tricycle, riding along between lanes of rush hour traffic on Harry Hines. A motorist returned him to his hysterical mother, who promised he would henceforth be restricted to his own backyard on Vagas Street.

INDUSTRY AND GOVERNMENT USES

In the period after World War II, both the Everett family and the sorrel horses lived near industrial facilities. Some were right across the street from the rising medical buildings. In late 1953, the Polley Bros. and Verson Company completed a new building at 5206 Harry Hines for two businesses: Texas Tool Traders and Machine Products Co. The land was purchased for this purpose in 1945, 7.5 acres at a cost of $15,000. Parkland Hospital was already under construction across the street. The westward movement of hospital uses did not discourage the development of new industrial uses.

Both businesses moved from locations on Ross Avenue, and both were forced to declare bankruptcy in the 1970s. Until 1960, Texas Tools Traders ran daily newspaper advertisements about their tools for machine shops, major drilling, and heavy construction needs. They then opened a machine shop on site. During World War II, Machine Products Co. engaged in wartime manufacture of bomb cases. After 1945, when many war manufacturers scrambled to find a niche for continued production, they transitioned to a machine shop for making gears and other industrial parts.

Padgett Printing and Lithographing Company built a 22,000

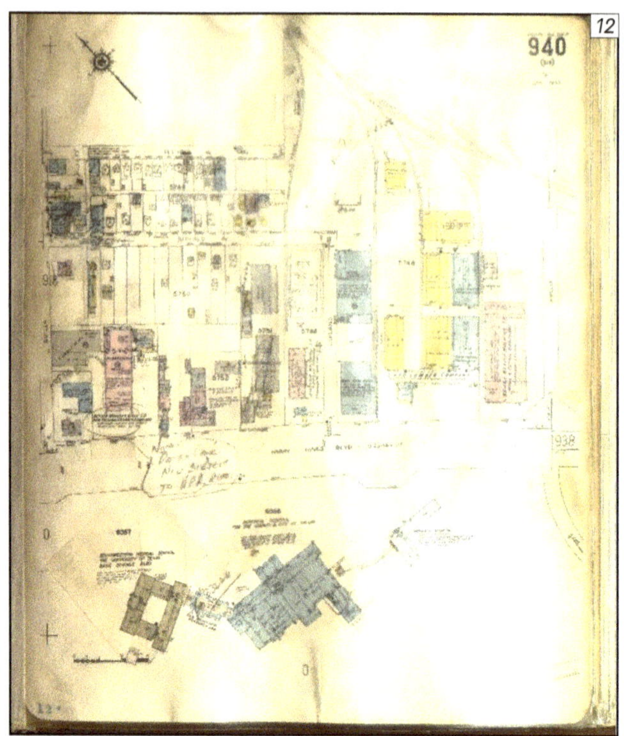

Figure 12: Industrial businesses across Harry Hines from the hospital, from 1953 Sanborn map used by fire insurance companies. Chet's Station and the Sinclair facility are on the right, Machine Products Co. next door. The handwritten note suggests that the Better Monkey Grip Co. is subject to special insurance terms. Courtesy of the University of Texas at Arlington.

square foot plant at 5912 Harry Hines in 1951. Brothers Hal W. and Jay D. Padgett published booklets, magazines, and "fine color work" using the technology of lithography. It had been a Dallas business since 1903. The post-war boom compelled them to seek larger facilities on available land. The company operated there for only seven years before selling the site for non-industrial uses. This was a step toward reclaiming land for residential and medical uses. The printing building no longer exists.

A much larger and potentially noisier and more odiferous facility was mercifully located a bit further from the new hospital at 5101 Maple Avenue. The vast Mosher Steel Company fabricating plant occupied much of the triangle formed by Maple Avenue, the M.K.T. tracks and Amelia Street, just southeast of Inwood Road. The company had grown from a small Dallas family business, a four-man machine shop on Pacific Avenue started by Theo Mosher in 1885. From 1895 to 1927, they occupied a much larger site on South Lamar Street, before constructing this facility. The new location had easy access to rail transportation in an area with many other industrial plants. Neighbors in 1951 included a meat packing plant, battery manufacturer, and Canada Dry Ginger Ale bottling plant.

By 1927, much of their work involved the custom manufacture of steel columns and beams for buildings. That year, they made the frame for Neiman-Marcus' new store at Commerce and Ervay. In 1928, they fabricated a steel bridge for the M.K.T. railroad, the first Texas company to do so, ending dependence on distant bridge manufacturers. The company also made decorative steel work and parts for boilers.

Descendants of Theo Mosher and William S. Mosher Sr. and Jr. built an impressive enterprise. They had a second manufacturing facility in Houston by 1907. They participated in the national promotion of Dallas industry. Their employee teams were quite successful fielding winning teams in sandlot baseball clubs from the 1920s to the 1950s. No amount of success seems to have gained the Moshers' full entrance to the Dallas' high society. They are quite absent from the 1930 Blue Book and Social Record and no Mosher daughter made a debut at Idlewild in line with the daughters of Medical District pioneers. Hopefully wealth and a tradition of family success compensated. The family sold the site in 1973.

Figure 13: This photograph was taken to document drainage issues in the area. Part of the Moshers' modern building is visible on the left, while the running remnants of the old creeks and riverbeds were visible in ditches on their property and other nearby land. Courtesy of the Dallas Public Library, Dallas History and Archives.

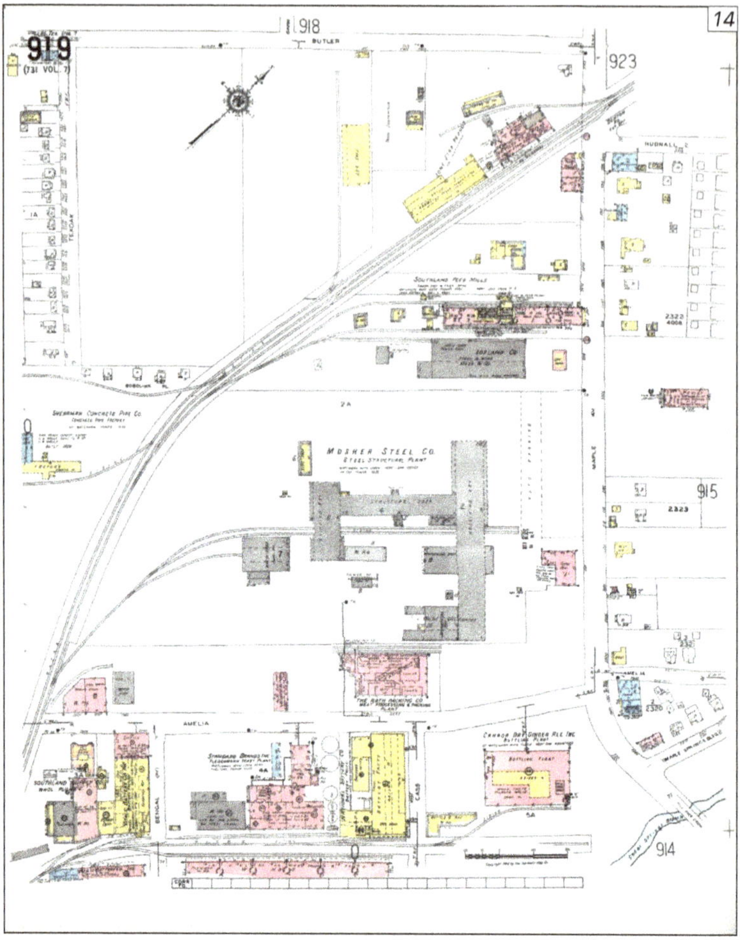

Figure 14: The Mosher Steel building and its neighbors, from the 1952 Sanborn map. The rail line is seen at the top right. Neighboring buildings are delineated with the common pink, yellow, and blue, indicating construction using brick, wood frame, and concrete respectively. The Mosher building is gray to indicate the use of light, inexpensive metal construction that could enclose a large operation. Courtesy of the Library of Congress.

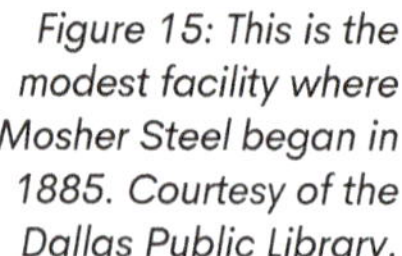

Figure 15: This is the modest facility where Mosher Steel began in 1885. Courtesy of the Dallas Public Library.

THIS IS LARGEST PNEUMATIC COMPACTOR EVER BUILT IN TEXAS

The Shovel Supply Company of 4900 Harry Hines Boulevard, built this monstrous pneumatic compaction roller designed for pressing down of airport runways, dams and other such work. L. C. Ferguson, owner of the company, says this is the largest pneumatic compactor ever built in this state. It was built for Atlas Construction of New York City. The compactor weighs 7,700 pounds empty. Its ballasted weight is 400,-000 pounds. Overall length is forty-six feet, seven-and-one-half inches. L. H. Bennett, sales manager of the company, shown in the picture said the compactor was built in thirty-six days. The 15-horsepower engine on the deck on which Bennett is standing is to power a hydraulic ram. This ram is used for testing the density of soil. The compactor was designed by Warren Kiser, engineer for Shovel Supply.

Figure 16: The Shovel Supply Company engineered and produced heavy equipment for industry. People at the time were surprised that one of its co-founders and co-owners was a woman, Miss Elsa Florence von Seggern, who thoroughly understood every aspect of the business.[1] Along with private industry, they contracted with the federal government on defense work. In 1952, their plant at 4900 Harry Hines produced this pneumatic compactor of immense size. It compacted the soil for road and dam building and was commissioned by a New York firm. Courtesy of The Dallas Morning News.

---

1 Tolbert, Frank X., "Miss Von Seggern's Business Saga," *The Dallas Morning News*, January 22, 1957, p. 1.

NEW HOME—One of Dallas County's 450 automatic voting machines is moved into its new $40,000 home near Harry Hines Boulevard at Industrial by R. H. (Bob) Clinger, right, and J. R. Hayden, assistant county engineer. The huge corrugated steel warehouse was built after the county ran out of room in which to store the half million dollars worth of voting machines.

Figure 17: The new steel warehouse cost the county $40,000. Courtesy of The Dallas Morning News.

The county government found the Medical District useful for two special uses: voting machine storage and a new home for juvenile offenders. Both were located at 4711 Harry Hines, at Amelia. In 1947, the county built a corru–gated metal Quonset hut as a warehouse at the rear of the property. In it they stored 450 automatic voting machines. A recount for a county commissioner's race in 1952 required officials to journey to the hut to search the machines. By 1954, the machines had grown to 525 in number, but the roof leaked, and they suffered without air conditioning and heat. County Judge Lew Sterrett refused to coddle the machines, saying their metal hut was adequate.

In front of that, the county built a bond-funded home for juvenile offenders. They were previously housed in the County Records Building, which had jail cells on the upper floors. The facility followed new ideas about the reform of so-called "juvenile delinquents," who were often considered the products of bad parenting. Once located far from adult prisoners, they would be reformed through counseling, educational, and recreational programming. The new facility provided a much better situation for them. Nobody initially asked if such a use would be incompatible with the planned new location of Parkland Hospital next door, but it later became an issue.

Figure 18: The company advertised their new building on the inside cover of the 1955 Dallas City Directory.

Figure 19: The Dallas County Juvenile Depart–ment moved from the downtown Records Building to the new location on April 1, 1951. Courtesy of the Dallas Public Library.

TREE PLANTING—Members of the Lakewood Garden Club gathered at the Juvenile Detention Home on Harry Hines Wednesday to plant a red oak tree. Left to right, are Mrs. J. Francis Middleton, chairman of the project; Mrs. Louis O. Moorman, standing by the tree, and Mrs. J. H. Hogue, kneeling. In addition, they planted twelve dozen red cannas, twenty-five dozen blue and purple iris and an assortment of early blooming spring bulbs.

Figure 20: Among the many volunteers who helped with the new facility were these ladies from the Lakewood Garden Club, seen here planting a donated tree. Courtesy of the Dallas Public Library.

In 1952, a young man the press called a "14-year-old Houdini" escaped from the home four times. He stole a car, his favorite act among his many crimes, and drove to Greenville.[2] In a much more serious event, the home also held sixteen-year-old John Michael Hawkins in 1951, as he awaited trial for the murder of his father. The accused admitted shooting oil executive Wallace E. Hawkins in their home on Strait Lane because of constant arguments about the boy's late hours.[3] Declared a juvenile delinquent by Juvenile Judge Dallas Blankenship, the younger Hawkins was ordered sent to the State School for Boys at Gatesville.

The P. C. Cobb Stadium is a much more fondly remembered city institution. When it was dedicated in 1939, it was called the Dallas High School Athletic Field and was inaugurated by short football games featuring the six top high school teams. It was built by the Works Progress Administration as a New Deal project, in a severe Art Deco style. The concrete stadium held 26,000 spectators. It came to be called the Dal-Hi stadium by the fans and drew fans from across the city. In 1957, it was renamed in honor of P. C. Cobb, who served forty-three years as athletic director for the Dallas Independent School District.

He was a driving force in erecting this centralized athletic facility for use by all the schools. The original cost was modest, and the stadium was so successful at attracting crowds and selling concessions

---

2   "Slippery Lad Held at Last, Police Hope," in *The Dallas Morning News*, July 30, 1952, p. 1.
3   Hand, Ken, "W. E. Hawkins, Oil Executive, Slain by Son, 16," in *The Dallas Morning News*, Aug. 6, 1951, p. 1.

Figure 21: The concrete architecture included relief panels depicting athletes at play. The panels were removed and preserved prior to the building's demolition. They are stored by the Dallas Department of Parks and Recreation in anticipation that they may find a new use. Courtesy of the Dallas Public Library and Willis Winters.

Figure 22: Concrete relief panel.

that its bond debt was soon paid in full. Both the playing field and dressing rooms set a new standard for such a facility. Two generations of Dallasites saw memorable feats of football magic there.

Like other fabulous new structures, it eventually aged and became less impressive. It was built on the site of the settling basin of the old Turtle Creek water treatment plant. The land was still owned by the city's water department. In 1979, Trammel Crow purchased the land. The stadium was torn down for the construction of the Infomart, in support of the growing wholesale trade center along Stemmons Freeway. Once again, the old made way for a new vision near the Medical District.

Figure 23: The original shape of the settling basin was still visible in this 1947 image, along with the old channel of the river. Courtesy of the Dallas Public Library.

Highway Beautification

by Robert Prejean

The dynamics of highway beautification is more than enhancing beautiful vistas with pretty trees and flowers and hoping the plants will survive. It comes down to community values desiring safe and visually pleasing roadway spaces overcoming the forces of land development and commercialism and whether there is a political will to protect and enhance such natural and aesthetically pleasing amenities.

During the late 19th and early 20th centuries, American communities had been embracing the City Beautiful movement of reforming cities to be scenic and magnificent. This was a time when new professions in city planning and landscape architecture came into greater acceptance. Beginning in the early 1900s, the automobile age took hold of Americans. At the

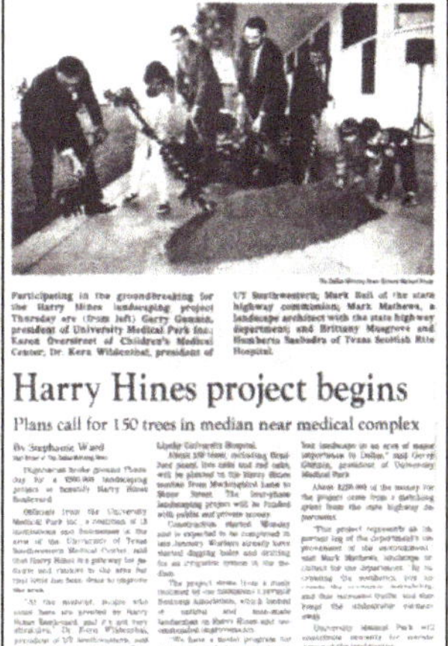

Courtesy of the Dallas Morning News.

time, these motorized vehicles were hailed for their ease of movement, but also as a health solution for replacing the carriages and wagons drawn by animals. Their urine, manure droppings, and resulting dust befouled local streets and breezed into homes and businesses. Instead of being limited to a walking distance from a set trolley line or the clip-clop of a hooved animal, automobiles allowed people freedom to roam as far as a good road would take them—a limiting factor in those early years of the automobile.

The automobile age wasn't just limited to the United States. Some European countries such as Germany were fascinated by this motorized innovation and the need for facilities to move about greater distances with ever increasing speeds. This need for speed led to the Germans' early creation of the autobahn and what would one day evolve into the American Interstate Highway System. Some early parkways in the United States embraced beauty as part of the linear road experience, including the Bronx River Parkway and Taconic Parkway in New York and Mount Vernon Memorial Parkway in Virginia.

Acceptance to beautify the fledging federal highway system was noted in a June 3, 1928 *Dallas Morning News* story titled, "Roads to Have Trees Planted." The role of the federal government's road building policy was expanded from just "appropriating only for the roadbed and directly kindered construction operations" to also include planting and maintenance of shade trees. American Motorist Association President J. Borton Weeks was quoted saying, "The planting and maintenance of shade trees along the Federal aid highway system of the United States will add materially to the joys of motoring and will be welcomed by the millions of motorists who use the highways daily."

Campaigns soon began for better roads, both locally and nationally. Automobile clubs working with local chamber of commerce groups were formed in cities across the nation to improve city and county roads plus work with distant communities to link highway improvements via "named highways." According to Jeff Dunn's Spring 2000 article in *Legacies: A History Journal for Dallas and North Central Texas*, these included such local roads as the Bankhead Highway from Washington, D.C. to San Diego, California; Dixie Overland Highway from Savannah, Georgia to San Diego, California; Exall Highway from Denison, Texas to Galveston, Texas; and the Dallas-Canadian-Denver Highway from Denver, Colorado to Galveston, Texas. The latter highway used what was then known as the Denton Road, which consisted of portions of either Lemmon Avenue or Maple Avenue. At the same time, garden clubs and road builders were sitting at the same table working to promote better roads and highways that were attractive.

More road improvements meant there were more people hitting the highways, and soon other forces were at work taking advantage of a captive audience of fast moving drivers along linear ribbons of concrete and asphalt. The halcyon landscapes along the highways were giving way to the clutter of billboards, automobile junk yards, and rickety buildings distracting drivers' attention and risking their safety, as was reported in a May 24, 1931 *Dallas Morning News* story about goals by the American Automobile Association to address the beautification of highways and regulation of roadside businesses.

Even before the opening of Harry Hines Boulevard, there was a strong desire to make this U.S. Highway 77 corridor an attractive northwest entry into the city of Dallas and avoid the commercialization found along Maple Avenue, the existing northwest road for U.S. Highway 77. A September 5, 1941, news story in *The Dallas Morning News* reported that Dallas City Plan Engineer E.A. Wood was making plans to plant trees along the new highway's shoulders and landscape the median; however, the same story noted a zoning change from residential to retail business along the new highway that the City Plan Commission recommended but was opposed by Mr. Wood as it would deter from the desired beautification of the roadway. Weeks later, the beautification of Harry Hines Boulevard was urged in a September 26, 1941 editorial in *The Dallas Morning*

Roads to Have Trees Planted

Highway Beautification Provided For by Federal Act.

Special to The News

WASHINGTON, June 2.—Beautification of the highways of the United States now looms as a possibility which may be realized within a comparatively short span of years as the result of the Federal highway act providing for the planting and maintenance of shade trees along the Federal aid highway system, it was announced by the American Motorists' Association.

An amendment to the act provides that specifications for Federal aid projects hereafter may include planting and maintenance of shade trees, this step being the first distinct departure from a Federal policy of appropriating only for the roadbed and directly kindered construction operations. The amendment to the act is regarded by proponents of highway beautification as one of the greatest strides yet taken toward making the highways of the United States traffic lanes of distinct attraction.

"The planting and maintenance of shade trees along the Federal aid highway system of the United States will add materially to the joys of motoring and will be welcomed by the millions of motorists who use the highways daily," President J. Borton Weeks of the motoring organization declared.

"Though years may be required to bring the highways of this country to that plane of tree-lined beauty already achieved on the vast vistas of traffic arteries in Europe, this amendment starts the Nation toward accomplishment of true beautification of its highways —something long desired by every American motorist."

Two other amendments to the Federal aid highway act, agreed upon by the House and Senate at the same time, provided for full financing of primary Federal aid projects and secondary feeders to the primary roads in areas of public lands in States where population averages ten or less persons a square mile, and also provided that the system of Federal aid highways eligible for expenditure of Federal funds in any State may exceed 7 per cent of the total highway mileage of such State on roads within national forests, Indian or other Federal reservations.

Courtesy of the Dallas Morning News.

News with the heading, "Inviting Approaches." The editorial noted the need to preserve the natural beauty of the roadsides and mentioned the work of Mrs. Jerry Stilwell as the chair of the citizens district committee for roadside improvements, writing letters and urging property owners along the new highways to organize and prevent billboards and unattractive structures. The new Harry Hines Boulevard corridor was the focus of the editorial, noting property owners would "profit immeasurably" if the highway corridor's beautification plan was supported by them, and warned, "If they permit unsightly signs and structures to mar this project, the value of their land will be depreciated, and Dallas will lose 50 per cent of the value of this new asset." Whether that zoning change request was approved or not, others were over time and results have shaped the road's character.

The opening of North Stemmons Freeway (IH-35E) in the early 1960s was a knock-out blow to the businesses lining the Harry Hines Boulevard corridor as traffic transitioned away from the older style highway and its clutter to the new limited access freeway passing through open undeveloped lands. The boulevard's once thriving motels, restaurants, and convenience stores either closed or evolved to dubious activities. Over time, the name Harry Hines Boulevard became synonymous with prostitution and the shabbier side of the city. Around the late 1980s and into the 1990s, civic leaders with the Stemmons Corridor Business Association and the University Medical Park Incorporated joined forces to address the landscape along Harry Hines Boulevard. As noted in a *Dallas Morning News* article from November 16, 1990, the plan got underway with $500,000 of public and private funds spent landscaping and planting 150 trees down the median between West Mockingbird Lane and Motor Street (today's Medical District Drive). Enhanced pedestrian crosswalks and an irrigation system were installed to sustain the improvements.

Thirty plus years later, these "legacy trees" of red oaks and live oaks provide welcome shade along the broad Harry Hines Boulevard median, while the Bradford pear trees look a little bedraggled. Building off the efforts of earlier civic leaders, the Harry Hines Boulevard corridor will undergo its next renaissance through the work of the Texas Trees Foundation in collaboration with the Southwestern Medical District. City, county, and regional planners are working together to enhance and improve the road corridor into a campus drive that addresses the health and human needs of all users in the Medical District. As the second largest employment center in the city of Dallas, the Medical District will continue to become denser with additional employees and residents. The Harry Hines urban streetscape and park design and implementation project will transform the Boulevard corridor into a safe, healthy, and healing corridor that encourages walking and biking, traffic calming, placemaking, and extensive plantings to cool the local environment and be inviting to all users.

THE HEART OF THE MEDICAL DISTRICT:
HARRY HINES BOULEVARD AND INWOOD ROAD

Standing at the corner of Harry Hines and Inwood, the modern Dallasite sees a major intersection of a thriving city. Early Dallasites could never have imagined that might happen. Surveyors were the first to knowingly stand at that corner, not as an inter-section but as the southern point of Miles Bennett's landholding. When Sam Street drew his map of Dallas in 1900, this was a corner formed by minor wagon roads passing through farmland. Just north-east of the juncture was the Wheeler store, doubtless a one-room building or even part of Mr. Wheeler's house, where he sold some goods to the isolated farmers in the region.

[Intersection from Sam Street map, intersection and Wheeler store called out.]

The land was purchased from Miles Bennett by Gabriel Knight and became part of the family's vast holdings. In the early 1900s, the area remained outside the city limits and the streets did not have official names recognized by the postal service. Lacking addresses, houses in such areas were described by how far they were from the court-house on a specified rural delivery route. The intersection was three and a half miles out on Rural Route No. 6. The earliest street names applied to Harry Hines were Bennett and Grauwyler, sometimes spelled "Garwheeler" in keeping with the proper pronunciation of the frontier family. Inwood was first called Maple Lawn Avenue, as it connected to the rapidly developing Oak Lawn area and Maple Avenue. By 1936 when Grauwyler reached northward to better con-nect Dallas to Farmers Branch, Denton and beyond, that section was named the Northwest Highway Connection.

Early plans for civic and residential development at the corner failed. The northern corner was particularly beset by grand plans that never materialized. In 1890, the city purchased that quadrant as park-land from Captain Alexander C. Lemmon, namesake for Lemmon Avenue. The planned Forest Park was referred to as being in North Dallas. It was crossed by the Knights Branch, which would have been a nice water feature for the park. The city did not move forward with the park, but the KATY Railroad did institute a Forest Park Station with trains running from downtown. This was proposed to serve new industry planned for the area, and likely let families from the city visit the countryside.

Figures 24 and 25: In 1958, some homes were located in the southeastern quadrant of the intersection of Harry Hines and Inwood, where they would eventually be in the way of expansion by Southwestern Medical School. The houses (right) were located on Hines. One of them still had an outhouse. Courtesy of the Dallas Public Library, Dallas History and Archives.

In 1899, a proposed new housing development appropriated the park name. The plan filed with the county for the Subdivision of Forest Park showed new secondary streets that would define four blocks of eight lots each. This plan was filed by the National Bank of Commerce. R.E.L. Knight was a trustee of that bank, so the family still had an interest in the land. The development did not come to fruition, though the streets were built and given to the city.[4]

Through the Depression and the war, only a few residences had addresses in the area along Inwood. At the war's end, the city made plans to build up the parcel, but made no progress. One plan was to widen Inwood to four lanes, making a boulevard that would connect to Northwest Highway. It was not fully realized. The northern side of the intersection is included in city plans to promote residential suburbs to answer post-war housing needs. The languishing Forest Park subdivision would be Forest Estates and Tex-Oak subdivisions. A shopping village across Inwood was also planned. In 1955, all plans were abandoned, and the apparently cursed Forest Park land once again failed to blossom into a residential district. It remained minimally utilized and passed through corporate and bank ownership for decades. In 1984, it was donated to the John D. and Catherine T. MacArthur Foundation of Illinois. From there, it became available by donation for the North Campus expansion of UT Southwestern Medical Center.

---

4   For more on this area of the Medical District, see Duane E. Peter, Donna Shepard and Steven M. Hunt, *An Evaluation of the Potential Presence of Historic Properties Located Within the North Campus Expansion Area of the University of Texas Southwestern Medical Center*, Dallas, Texas, Miscellaneous Report of Investigations Number 64, Geo-Marine, Inc., 1993.

A post-war effort to build a Veterans Hospital at the intersection also failed. In 1947, the Veterans Administration bought seventeen acres of land from the Southwestern Medical Foundation for the hospital. The existing veterans' facility was south of Dallas in Lisbon, a community along South Lancaster Road. It was old and small. The new one would take advantage of proximity to the planned Southwestern Medical School to train military doctors and access shared staff and medical personnel.

Many praised this plan, including veterans in organizations such as the American Legion. Others opposed it. Some opponents said they did "not want to be guinea pigs for medical students." Ongoing national conversations praised and valued veterans after the recent victory. Some voices were equally worried that the government would provide those veterans with too much support and encourage lack of initiative in young men. There was also support for keeping military services within military institutions.

In response, the VA abandoned the plan for a location in the District in favor of a large new addition at the Lisbon location. The federal government owned the land in the District, and in 1951, they proposed a government office building for the site.

City leaders and the Southwestern Medical Foundation were both opposed. If the government chose to sell the land, it would bring the highest price from a buyer intent on building an industrial facility. City leaders feared that such a sale would harm the planned new Parkland Hospital. For this reason, in January 1952 they quickly annexed land around the Parkland site, including the federal land, so they could zone it to exclude industry. The immediate threat forced the city to finally make a significant move toward claiming the future District lands for non-industrial uses. Negotiations and accusations ensued. In 1952, the foundation agreed to a land-swap compromise that would return the land to them without financial loss. All the land involved was used for medical expansion over the years, but the Veterans Hospital lost the opportunity to be part of the growing Medical District.

Since that period, advances in medical technology have caused repeated expansion of facilities. By the dawn of the twenty-first century, hospital facilities surrounded the intersection, reaching all the way to Mockingbird Lane and Maple Avenue. Only the eastern quadrant retained two blocks of commercial use right at the corner.

Harry Hines the man is not often discussed in twenty-first century Dallas. In many minds, his name came to mean an area of vice, wholesale import warehouses open to the public, and a few beloved restaurants. Hines is remembered in a small tree-shaded triangular park where North Harwood and Ashland Streets intersect with the southern limits of Harry Hines Boulevard. The park is named for him and contains a marker erected by his many friends in 1956. It notes his years serving on the Texas Highway Commission and his vision that created the divided highway that ultimately carried his name. What was once a breathtakingly wide and beautiful new highway is now seen as a fairly standard example of a major city road. This one is special, to all of the people who lived, worked, and were healed along its route.

Chapter 5

RESIDENTIAL DEVELOPMENTS

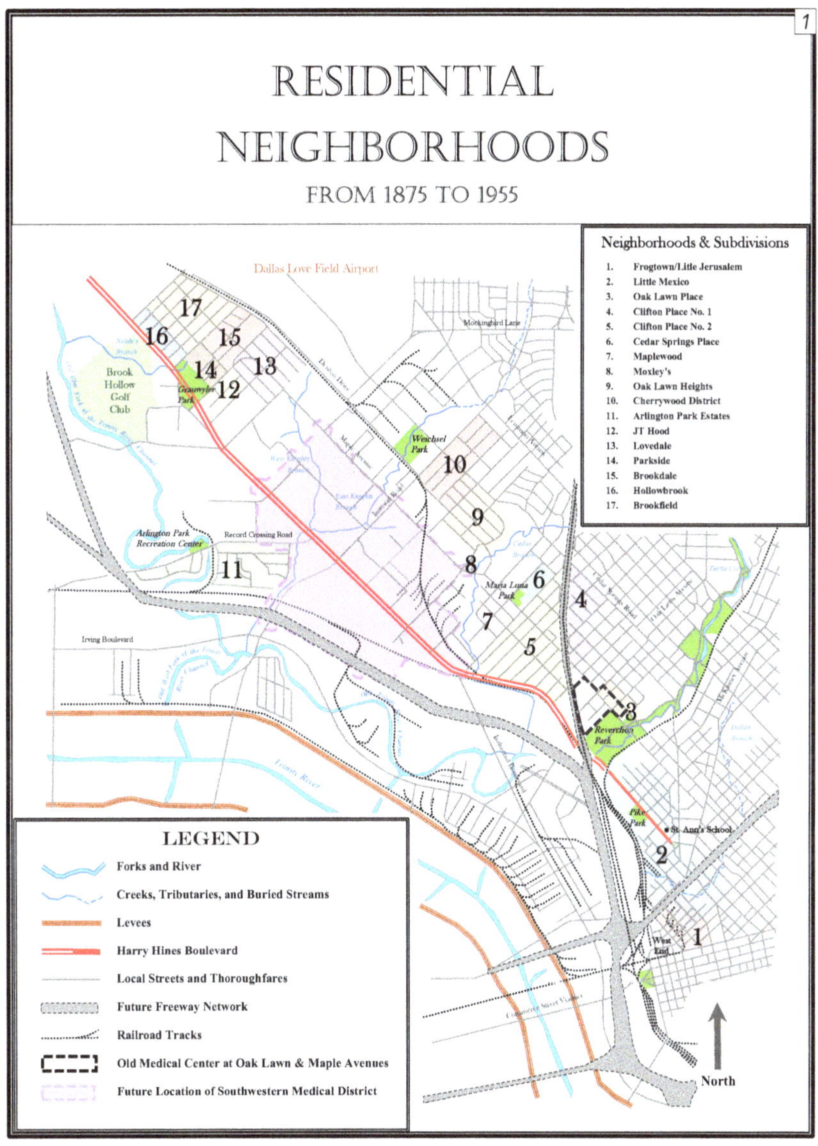

Figure 1: Map of the residential areas in the Medical District lands. Courtesy of Robert Prejean.

Residential development of the rural lands northwest of downtown was slow and limited, but the idea was in place by 1900. Land along Oak Lawn easily attracted higher-end home building. That area was chosen by successful children of the pioneers, including Obadiah Knight's son Epps. Oak Lawn Heights is an excellent example of such a neighborhood. It is located just northeast of the District, between Maple and Cedar Springs, south of Hudnall. The new neighborhood enjoyed easy access by road and the new Dallas-Denton interurban line. This development was intended for residents of upper-middle-class means. Homes were required to be built of brick. Images of homes constructed there were published in the papers, including the eight-room English cottage for the Valentine family at Parkland Avenue and Cedar Springs Boulevard. Development along such transportation lines, termed "streetcar suburbs," was common in the early 20th century. The success of those housing developments was so dependent on the availability of easy transportation that the neighborhood developers and streetcar lines sometimes worked together. Further toward the river within the Medical District, the long-distance rail lines had a completely opposite effect. They made access difficult.

Originally, few crossings with the rails were grade separated, meaning either the rail or the city street crossed above the other on a bridge. Cars and buses had to watch for trains and wait for them to pass. Thus, both routine delays and danger of collision were added to the unappealing noise and pollution of living near railroads.

LITTLE MEXICO

Little Mexico grew organically amid existing settlement and answered a specific housing need of new immigrants. The original boundaries of the neighborhood are irregular. Its southernmost part begins near the West End, and it extends generally north-westward to Reverchon Park. It reaches up to the edge of Klyde Warren Park, and then northward to a small extension between Uptown and Turtle Creek Parkway. Industrial uses to its west included a Magnolia Petroleum distribution facility, the Neuhoff Brothers meat packing plant, grain silos, and a steam plant. These might provide employment opportunities but were otherwise not desirable neighbors.

The area was originally settled by an earlier immigrant group: Jewish people fleeing oppression in Russia and Eastern Europe. They arrived slightly before and after 1900, and most arrived with little money. They had no choice but to settle in a less desirable part of Dallas. The southernmost part of Little Jerusalem, nearest the West End, included the former legal prostitution haven, Frogtown. The ramshackle homes were already old, as were the accommodations just to the north, though they were of better construction.[1]

The new residents settled in and established temples and businesses. As they began to prosper, some moved out to newer neighborhoods. After 1910, a new group of residents fleeing the violence of the Mexican Revolution arrived. Earlier Jewish immigrants had struggled to earn their living amid anti-Semitism, but the newcomers initially found themselves even more limited to low-paying labor.

By 1919, the balance of the population in the neighborhood had shifted, with most of the Jewish residents moving to new areas. The Dallas Mexican American Historic League (DMAHL), many of whose leaders grew up in Little Mexico, identifies it as "El Barrio," the mother neighborhood in Dallas for those living in other barrios near other employment centers, such as Cement City.[2]

The term "Little Mexico" was first used by *The Dallas Morning News* in 1919, in two articles.[3] Both give insight into how the rest of Dallas saw the community. In July, a clean-up campaign was announced, where public health officials would examine all food-selling establishments in the neighborhood, to verify sanitary habits. This was not yet a practice common for establishments citywide. It was an insulting, targeted effort. In August, authorities moved in to examine private residences and remove anything they deemed to be trash. Even St. Paul Hospital's charitable Marillac Clinic in Little Mexico, which was beneficial to the people, was based on negative stereotypes about the inhabitants. It was a response to perceptions that the neighborhood might pose a health hazard to the city, incubating disease.

Meanwhile, the residents built a thriving community. They established numerous religious organizations, sometimes in the former Jewish temples. They defeated their limited employment opportunities

---

1   For further information on the history of Jewish people in Dallas, see Rose G. Biderman, *They Came to Stay: The Story of the Jews of Dallas, 1870–1997*, (Austin: Eakin Press, 2001) and Gerry Cristol, *A Light in the Prairie: Temple Emanu-El of Dallas 1872–1997*, (Fort Worth, TX.: Texas Christian University, 1998.)

2   See the organization's website at https://www.dmahl.org to read about their research and exhibits. See also a work by one of DMAHL's founding members, Sol Villasano, *Dallas's Little Mexico*, (Charleston: Arcadia Publishing, 2011).

3   "Clean-Up Campaign for 'Little Mexico' District," *The Dallas Morning News*, July 13, 1919, p. 9.

by starting their own businesses. These mostly served the community needs, but some grew into city-wide sales, such as the Luna Tortilla Factory. Mike Martinez opened the first El Fenix restaurant in 1918, on McKinney Avenue, starting a family dynasty. Neighborhood entrepreneurs and craftsmen offered all sorts of retail and services, including shoe repair, barber shops, and funeral services. By 1920, an estimated 6,000 people of Mexican heritage lived in the neighborhood.

St. Ann's School became the cultural center of the neighborhood. Its first building was constructed in 1927, adjacent to the existing Our Lady of Guadalupe Church. By 1946, it included an elementary and high school, as well as community center, all intended to educate and to retain the residents in the Catholic faith. The third Bishop of Dallas, Joseph P. Lynch, recognized the need for such a facility in Little Mexico, and his efforts created an important local institution.

By 1920, residents began forming fraternal and civic organizations to help the people of the community. The Spanish-American Alliance and local chapters of the Woodmen of the World were fraternal mutual aid societies, which collected funds and used them to help people in times of need. Such organizations have historically been used as a form of insurance for immigrant communities of modest means. The community also instituted sports teams, Spanish-language newspapers, and aid societies based within the churches. Residents and businesses tended to stay at the same place during the 1920s and 1930s, adding an element of stability to the community.[4]

Figure 2: Some Little Mexico businesses, such as the Luna Tortilla Factory and El Fenix, grew into large operations known throughout the city. They also promoted an appreciation for Mexican cuisine to the entire city population. Courtesy of the Dallas Public Library.

---

4   Bailon, Gilbert, *Little Mexico: An Enduring Hub of Mexican Culture in Dallas*, (Arlington, TX.: UTA history department, research project, 1991), p. 10. For the history of the area, with many images, see Sol Villasana, *Dallas's Little Mexico*, (Mount Pleasant, SC.: Arcadia Publishing, 2011).

Figure 3: Many smaller businesses serve neighborhood needs.
Photographs from the Zambrano Studio documented happy occasions
in the neighborhood, capturing the joy of brides, new babies, and
smiling extended families. Courtesy of the Dallas Public Library.

Pike Park, originally Summit Park, became another center of community life, but only after an ugly period when Mexican Americans were excluded from using it. The original Summit Park was forbidden until 1931. Even children were expected to walk around the grounds rather than through the park reserved for whites. When the park was opened to the people of Little Mexico, they embraced it as the location for celebrations of all types, Cinco de Mayo, the Fourth of July, and El Diez y Seis de Septiembre. The park has been called "the neighborhood's collective soul and epicenter." In the 1970s, as the formerly cohesive community intruded upon by outside interests and residents began to move away, the city worked with residents to renovate the park in hopes that it could remain a cultural heritage center for the Mexican American population as they moved to other neighborhoods.

Through the 1950s, Little Mexico remained a fairly homogenous community. Whenever they ventured away from their barrios, Mexican Americans risked humiliating racist encounters, such as being refused service in stores or restaurants. Outsiders continued to view Little Mexico and its residents negatively and to limit their success.

A watershed moment for Mexican Americans in Dallas occurred in Little Mexico in 1973. Police searching for suspects in a minor robbery removed Santos Rodriguez, aged twelve, and his brother David from their home and questioned them in a police car. While threatening Santos with a loaded gun, one of the officers fatally shot him.

This act stirred people to public protest. The March of Justice for Santos Rodriguez at City Hall was spurred by this single event, but also expressed the frustration over years of unfair economic treatment, marginalization, and outright racism. The officer who killed Santos served only two-and-a-half years in jail. The incident and the resulting protest spurred changes in the police department and opened opportunities for Mexican Americans in local politics. None of that could bring much comfort to Santos' family.

Little Mexico was one of the many neighborhoods to be physically and socially divided by new roads built to accommodate increased automobile traffic. Nationally and in Dallas, most such destruction began after World War II, but for Little Mexico, it started earlier. Damage to the neighborhood's cohesiveness began in 1937. The new Northwest Highway (Harry Hines) needed to use an existing street to connect to downtown. Planners chose Turney Avenue. It ran through the southern parts of Little Mexico and along the northeast edge of Pike Park. Homes and local businesses along Turney were sacrificed as it was widened to become Harry Hines.

Figure 4: Artist Charles T. Bowling captured this image of Little Mexico in 1936. Courtesy of Dallas Museum of Art.

Figure 5: A scene on Alamo Street in Little Mexico, in the early 1950s. City of Dallas Photographers Collection, Dallas Public Library, Dallas History and Archives.

Figure 6: The Dallas Times Herald captured the progress of the protesters as they moved toward city hall. The protest took place on July 28, 1973, two days after Santos' death. African Americans active in the Dallas movement for civil rights joined the protest. Dallas Times Herald Collection, Dallas Public Library, Dallas History and Archives.

As the war approached its end and planners looked to future transportation needs, an even worse blow to Little Mexico was conceived. The roadbed of the Cotton Belt Railroad ran from downtown toward Reverchon Park and along the western edge of the Park Cities. The line's cars could be rerouted, and that strip used for a new toll road. Post-war highways were often built on the route of old railroads. Any other route would have posed extreme difficulties in gathering enough land through older settled areas of cities.

The city was not able to open the new Dallas North Tollway between downtown and Loop 635 until 1968. It split Little Mexico in a way that the railroad never had. It was not the only minority or older neighborhood harmed by highways. The African American neighborhoods of Tenth Street and North Dallas Freedman's Town were split by Interstate 35 and Central Expressway. The Cedars neighborhood south of downtown was separated from it by Interstate 30.

None of this was accidental. State highway planners and civic leaders saw these neighborhoods as marginal, declining, full of dilapidated buildings and poverty. The goal of urban renewal was to replace such neighborhoods with planned housing that would promote prosperity — theoretically for the existing inhabitants, but usually more for wealthier parties. Highways were so obviously valuable at the time that they were difficult to argue against.

The damage was not just physical. Community ties and traditions that had helped people prosper were broken. Neighbors lost the ability and will to support each other. None of that was recognized, understood, or targeted, but it was vital to the people.

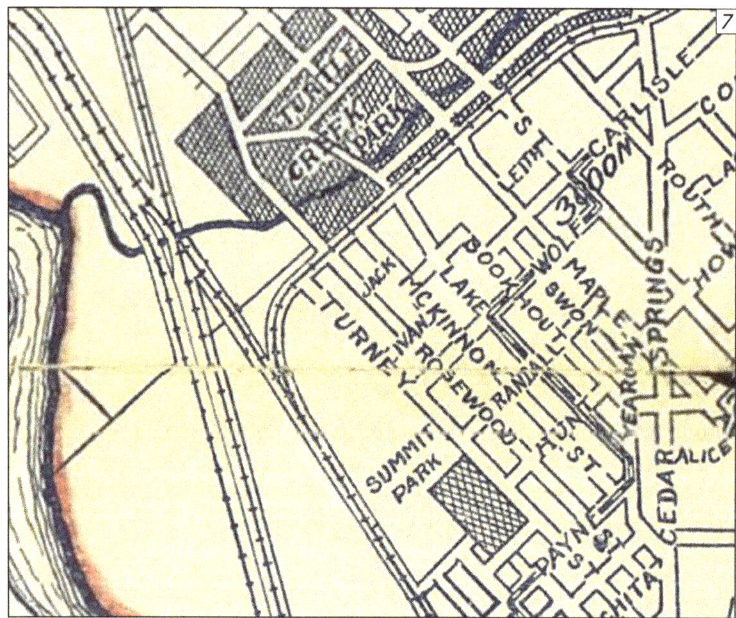

Figure 7: Turney Ave. before it became Harry Hines. Turtle Creek Park was renamed Reverchon Park and Summit Park became Pike Park. From the 1919 C. Weischel map. Courtesy of Old Red Museum.

Figure 8: The intersection of Turney Avenue and Payne Street in 1940. Retail buildings are on the left, with houses in the background. Workers are attending to electric lines while sitting on the lines. Courtesy of Dallas Mexican American Historical League.

Every year, less remains physically of Little Mexico. In early 2020, the house and grocery store of lifelong resident Charlie Villasana were demolished. These were probably the last representative buildings of Little Mexico. The DMAHL organization works to preserve barrio history through the preservation and exhibition of stories, photographs, and documents. The city of Dallas has supported maintaining Little Mexico's heritage at Pike Park and the renaming of its recreation center for Santos Rodriguez.

CLIFTON PLACE

The story of neighboring Clifton Place is much different. Col. William Edgar Hughes was a self-made man. He arrived in Dallas in 1873, already worth an impressive $17,000.

Working as a bank president, lawyer, and cattleman, he became the richest man in Dallas. He amassed 4,000 acres of land. In 1893, he was credited with helping Dallas dominate the production of registered Holsteins. His stock farm of 415 acres at the edge of the city limits was promoted as a tourist attraction. When Col. Hughes died in 1918, he left an estate valued at $500,000.

He named his ranch, his line of Holstein cattle, and his daughter "Clifton." It was his wife Annie's middle name. The cattle won $500

The Park
That Never Was

by Robert Prejean

"A horse, a horse! My kingdom for a horse," Shakespeare's King Richard III cried out. No doubt about it, we've all had similar days at work or home when we thought, If only? City leaders can find themselves in related states of disbelief when an event of great hope is suddenly snatched away. Over a century ago in Dallas, it was a large piece of land donated for park space. Today, we are left to deliberate *if only* with "if only they had known then."

Inside the October 13, 1914, edition of *The Dallas Morning News*, the headline proclaimed the city's good fortune.

SPLENDID DONATION
TO CITY OF DALLAS

COL. W. E. HUGHES GIVES
LARGE TRACT OF LAND
FOR PARK PURPOSES

CONDITIONS ACCEPTED

Colonel William Edgar Hughes would donate to the city 150+ acres of land to be used as park space. Such good news was welcomed by city leaders following the worst flooding in the city in 1908 plus a 1911 meningitis epidemic driving the need for a new, up-to-date hospital. City Beautiful initiatives for solving the ills impacting American cities were popular, and Dallas civic leaders hired landscape architect George E. Kessler to create the city's first master plan, a plan to address the city's health and safety through flood control, re-routing rail lines, boulevards, along with parks and open space.

Col. Hughes was a lawyer, banker, rancher, land developer, and visionary. A pillar in the Dallas business community, he took an active interest in the city he loved. In 1913, he even tried to persuade the city to relocate Parkland Hospital's replacement facility somewhere else to restore the hospital grounds as park land. Though he moved from Dallas in 1900, he continued to hold onto his Dallas farm—Clifton Farm—until near his death when it was platted as Clifton Place No. 1 and No. 2. The donation was a wonderful gift for Dallas, but it came with a few stipulations: (1) that the city purchase the Cole family's twenty-two acres to be combined with other public lands as park spaces commencing six months after the donation, (2) the right to pump water from Long's Lake for the benefit of his contiguous property to the east, and (3) within six months build a Maple Avenue underground crossing at the Missouri, Kansas, and Texas (KATY) Railroad to replace the existing dangerous grade crossing and steep curving dirt road. The city met the first two conditions, but the last condition was financially difficult for the city. Unable to meet the last condition, the donation was taken back.

Twenty years later, the Trinity River would be moved and contained within a levee system. In the 1960s, North Stemmons Freeway was built, and towards the end of the 20th century, the land once donated for park space and later withdrawn now contains the offices and showrooms of the Dallas Market Center, large hotels, plus entertainment. If only...or if only then city leaders knew what we know today.

The widening nature of Maple Avenue in early 20th century.
Source: From the collections of the Dallas History & Archives
Division, the Dallas Public Library.

in prizes at the 1889 Texas State Fair. The daughter married John W. Springer in June of 1891 at St. Matthew's Cathedral downtown. The couple later moved to Denver for her health and established a ranch there.

By 1900, the city was overtaking his once rural stock farm in what would become Oak Lawn and the edge of the Medical District. Col. Hughes did not get rich by failing to recognize an opportunity when it approached. He developed his ranch land into residential neighborhoods. The initial Clifton Place was offered to buyers as Dallas' newest and closest addition in 1913. It was a roughly triangular piece of land to the south and west of Cedar Springs Road and the Cotton Belt line.

Advertisements touted its high elevation and view of downtown, the quality residences nearby, and the likelihood of ever-increasing values. The advertisements included a picture of the Colonel himself. Clifton Heights was centered on Oak Lawn between Maple and Routh, reaching Turtle Creek and later renamed Oak Lawn Place.

Much of Col. Hughes' ranch became residential land of ever-increasing density and value. He donated some land for the purpose of creating a park near the later Reverchon Park, a lovely civic gesture. It was also an act guaranteed to promote lasting property values for his developments. He took the potential parkland back when the city did not fulfill promises to create grade separation for the Missouri, Kansas, and Texas (KATY) Railroad tracks. Unless the tracks were raised, Hughes' vision of a safe carriage path through the land could not be fulfilled. His vision for the initial Clifton Place was for an area of elegant homes, sculpted parkland, and visible wealth.

Not all of the Clifton lands were envisioned that way. Clifton Place Addition 2 was literally on the other side of the tracks, opening blocks of land between the Cotton Belt line and Harry Hines. Lots here were mostly sold in the mid to late 1920s, and this development seems to have been under the control of Col. Hughes' widow, Annie Clifton Hughes. The initial advertisements in 1922 offered lots priced from $200 to $900, with easy terms, starting with a $10 down payment. It seems aimed at buyers of modest income or at the early stages of their professional life, seeking an affordable but nice neighborhood. The houses, potentially viewed as starter homes for young couples, were modest in size, commonly with four rooms. It is the only Clifton development to still carry the name Clifton Place.

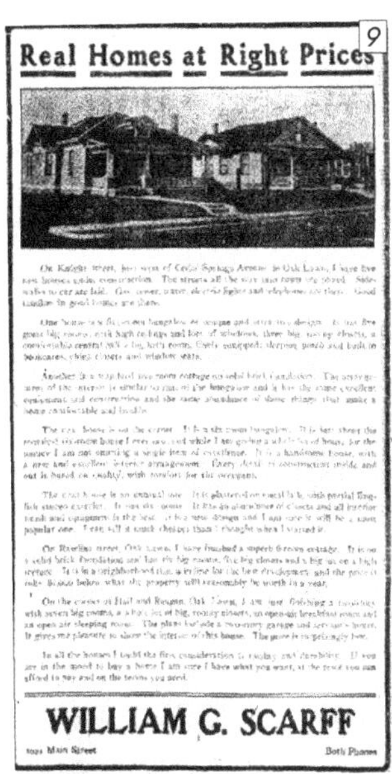

Figure 9: The original Clifton Place advertisements that ran in The Dallas Morning News in 1913. Courtesy of The Dallas Morning News. Figure 10: Regardless of Col. Hughes' original vision for Reverchon Park, it attracted users from beyond his development. It was a popular location for baseball, with a field and bleachers completed by 1924. Here we see a group from the Mexican Baptist Chapel enjoying a weenie roast in 1948. Dallas Mexican American Historical League.

This area was further from Oak Lawn and closer to the evolving Little Mexico. Land sales during the 1920s were to buyers with non-Spanish surnames, and later ownership may have remained fairly Anglo even as residents changed. By the 1950s and 1960s, city directories show a greater Mexican American representation, particularly on the streets to the southeast, such as Douglas. However, the neighborhood still had mixed occupation, allowing some opportunity for people of different cultures to mingle and meet.

Among the Mexican American descendants was Francisco "Pancho" Medrano. Born in 1920 in Little Mexico to hard-working immigrant parents, he experienced the pain of racism and segregation as a child. His parents' inability to provide costlier clothing for his attendance at Crozier Tech shortened his education. His subsequent job at a stone quarry taught him a skilled trade: making jigs for manufacturing. This skill led to employment at the North American Aviation plant and introduced him to the concept of union organization. As an organizer and later national leader in the United Auto Workers, he learned that people could gain a voice and change their circumstances through group effort and connections. He worked with national leaders including Cesar Chavez, participated in national civil rights activities, and met presidents Jimmy Carter and Lyndon B. Johnson.

He applied his knowledge to Dallas politics. Through his family store on Douglas in Clifton Place, he built a voting coalition of the previously marginalized Mexican American population. His children were the first to achieve elected office. The store became a center for political discussion and organizing citizens to register and vote.

Pancho's son Roberto led the way into elected office, beginning a thirteen-year stint as a Dallas ISD trustee in 1973. His brother Ricardo also broke a significant barrier when elected to the Dallas City Council in 1979. Daughter Pauline held the council seat from 2005 to 2013, and Francisco Junior's son Adam Medrano completed his term-limited eight-year service there in 2021. Members of the family continue to participate in political advocacy, community organizations, and causes related to education, parks, and the well-being of Dallas. Pancho and his wife Esperanza "Hope" Medrano both have elementary schools named for them, hers in Clifton Place, his north of Love Field.

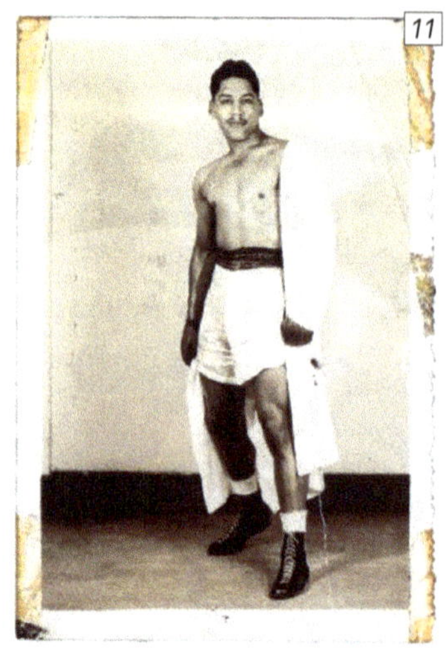

Figure 11: In his youth, Pancho Medrano participated in boxing through the Catholic Youth Association. Courtesy, Pancho Medrano Papers, Special Collections, The University of Texas at Arlington Libraries.

Figure 12: All of Medrano's past work was cited in his campaign to be the Sergeant at Arms for the UAW Local 645. Courtesy, Pancho Medrano Papers, Special Collections, The University of Texas at Arlington Libraries.

Figure 13: Pancho Medrano (center) with civil rights leaders Walter R. McMillan, Roosevelt Johnson, A. Maceo Smith, Harold E. Holly, Rev. G. T. Thomas and R. R. Revis opposing the poll tax in 1963.

OTHER RESIDENTIAL OFFERINGS IN THE MEDICAL DISTRICT

Nearby was another development of modest homes for workers on former agricultural land. The three small additions of Maplewood included areas along Kings Road and Lucas Drive, near Maple, the former property of the Kendall family. Maplewood was part of what *The Dallas Morning News* called a building boom in the early 1920s.

J. H. Power's company promoted the new subdivisions, with "Cottage Homes" priced under $2,000.[5] Each had two bedrooms and a sleeping porch. They warned of a coming shortage of "desirable homes" to encourage buyers. Mr. Power had been selling real estate since 1902. He changed his company name from Metropolitan Investment Company to Power Investment Company in 1917 and worked with the predominant Dallas real estate firm of Murphy & Bolanz. They proudly reported his accomplishment of selling 180 of his modest five-room cottages in various locations in 1921, which they thought contributed to productive citizenship among homeowners.[6] As with Clifton Place Addition 2, this neighborhood was close enough to Little Mexico that its residents eventually began to move in alongside the original settlers. In 1937, the Dallas Parks Department bought undeveloped land in Maplewood from four owners. The resulting park was later

---

5   Advertisement, *The Dallas Morning News*, Aug. 29, 1920, p. 14.
6   "Record for 1921," *The Dallas Morning News*, Jan. 1, 1922, p. 4. They noted that Power Investment Company sold one home every 48 hours.

Changing Community Character Along Maple Avenue

by Robert Prejean

Think of it as an urban relationship. A street corridor can define the neighborhoods that depend on it, and vice versa. Like most relationships, some identify with one another to form a long-term bond. Some are dysfunctional, and, without structure, just drift apart. And for some, the honeymoon is long over, each going through the motions and in need of counseling to sort things out and renew the flame. Together, they have their own urban life cycles, with changing needs, values, and outside influences.

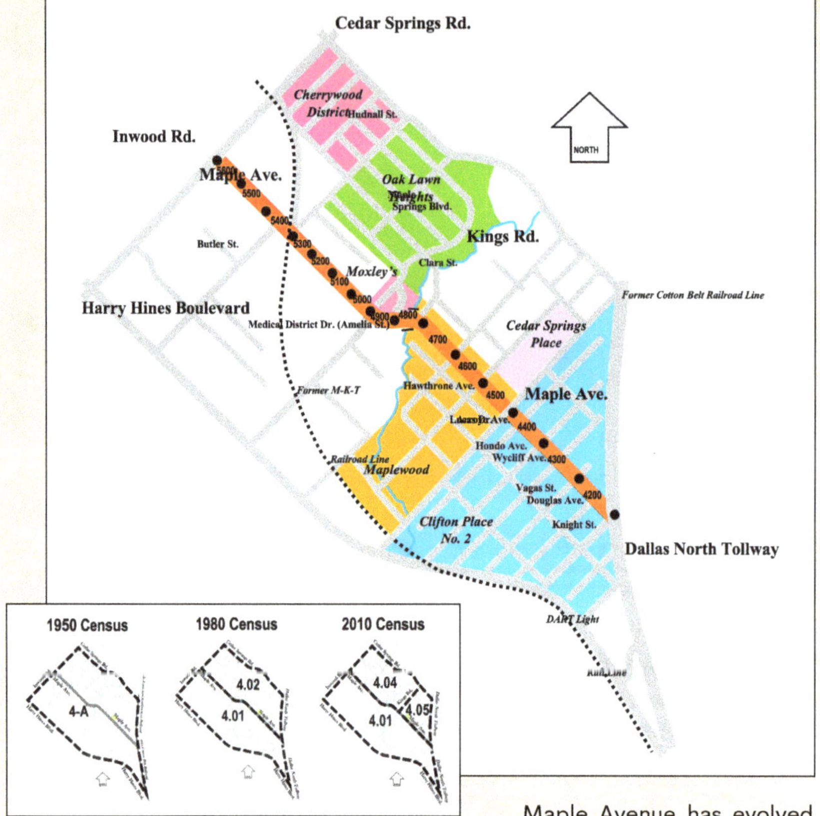

Maple Avenue has evolved as its uses and surroundings have changed with the growth of Dallas. Designated for years as U.S. Highway 77, the road served as the main northwest travel route leading to and from central Dallas until 1941. Maple Avenue functioned as a commercial corridor as nearby residential subdivisions blossomed along its edge from the 1920s through the early 1950s. The area bounded today by Cedar Springs Road, Inwood Road, Harry Hines Boulevard, and Dallas North Tollway and split in the middle by Cedar Springs Branch has six subdivisions—Clifton Place No. 2, Maplewood, and Cedar Springs Place south of the creek, and Moxley's, Oak Lawn Heights, and Cherrywood District north of the stream. For the 1950 Census, this area was designated Census Tract 4-A.

In 1950, this area was almost solid White at 98.9% of the population compared to the city of Dallas at 86.8%. It was a working-class community reflected in the percentage of residents' median family incomes plus, those with bachelor's degrees or higher, lower than that of the city. The corner of Maple and Lucas Drive was the community's center with a Safeway grocery store, Skillern & Sons drug store, Lucas Theater, plus a bakery, barber, sporting goods, and a couple of furniture shops all within walking distance. There was only one church along the Maple Avenue corridor. After World War II, most urban centers underwent change. Housing was hard to find, cars were faster, and expressways were a solution to open undeveloped lands to new suburban housing, while older single-family neighborhoods were rezoned to multi-family to increase the housing stock. The same held true for this area. Over the next thirty years, external events slowly impacted this area—Parkland Hospital's move to Harry Hines Boulevard, creation of Dallas' freeway network, Love Field Airport expansions, land use changes, and white flight.

Between 1950 and 2010, the area's population increased and was more diverse. By the 1960 Census, the geographic measures for this area would split in two—down Maple Avenue to become Tracts 4.01 and 4.02. The 1980 Census showed a clear population churn in percentage of racial make-up, with White dropping while Black and Other rose. Notable was the percentage population represented in a separate category termed Spanish Origin. By 1980, Maple Avenue appliance shops gave way to electronic and television stores, and while grocery stores were fewer, fast-food concerns filled local appetites. By 1990, what was Census Tract 4.02 split along Kings Road to become Tracts 4.04 and 4.05. Tract 4.04 remained mostly single family in character, while Tract 4.05 transitioned to multi-family complexes. With the 2010 Census, the combined area retained a diverse population mix, but most notable was the rise in the Asian category, with all three tracts well above the city's 2.9% share. By 2010, Maple Avenue had fewer liquor stores, bars, and lounges and slightly more grocery stores and pawn shops, and still only one church that continues to serve the community today.

named Maria Luna Park for the matriarch of the family behind the Luna Tortilla Factory.

The first public low-cost housing project in Dallas, and one of the first west of the Mississippi, was completed near the park in 1937. Cedar Springs Place, between Lucas Drive and Hawthorne Avenue, was at the northern tip of Clifton Place.

Construction of such projects began as a New Deal initiative in 1935. The mayor of Dallas went to Washington to plead Dallas' case for inclusion in the first round of construction and was successful. In keeping with the dominant southern tradition, the city applied for segregated projects. Cedar Springs Place was only for white occupants.

Figures 14 and 15: The modern buildings of Cedar Springs Place included balconies and new landscaping. They were arranged to form enclosed green space for the residents' use. Courtesy of the Dallas Public Library, Dallas History and Archives.

Housing program officials acquired the entire block of land for $66,000. The sellers, Mr. and Mrs. Fred White, were pictured in the newspaper looking understandably happy to make such a sale during the Depression.[7] The total cost of the project approached $1,000,000. It was designed as twenty-eight low-rise units, containing 181 apartments of three to five rooms. Tenants were chosen from 700 applicants. Landscaping was included but not well maintained over the years.

Along with stimulating the economy and creating jobs, the purpose of such projects was to clear older slum areas and provide housing in keeping with the latest views on health, safety, and proper living. Fireproof construction materials, such as concrete tile, were used at Cedar Springs Place. Kitchens were planned to ease the housewife's labor, bathrooms were included, and surfaces were durable and easily cleaned. This may or may not have created a pleasant interior environment, as such design can be quite dreary. The project is now listed on the National Register of Historic Places and continues to operate as housing.

---

7   "$66,000 Paid for Low-Cost Housing Site," *The Dallas Morning News*, Oct. 10, 1935, p. 15.

Figure 16: The Dallas Morning News *documented the first family that moved into Little Mexico Village. Maurice and Refugio Perez and their children took possession of a six-room apartment which rented for $18 a month. Its bathroom and kitchen facilities were a vast improvement over their previous residence. Courtesy of* The Dallas Morning News.

The city's first such project for African Americans was built in 1942 in east Dallas. A third community, restricted to people of Mexican descent, opened in Little Mexico that same year. Little Mexico Village's construction utilized modern methods of concrete construction. The finished peach color paid homage to the Mexican tradition of colorful buildings. The project offered apartments with some of the latest appliances, such as electric refrigerators, for about $13 per month. Move-in day photographs in *The Dallas Morning News* promoted the joyous delight of the residents. As the building aged, the apartments remained tenanted, and the Village took its place in the history and collective memory of the neighborhood.

The Cherrywood District was created by C. C. Weischel

Figure 17: The Dallas Housing Authority maintains ownership of the apartments, as well as its original bright color. Courtesy of Evelyn Montgomery.

on 400 acres of his own family's former country estate. He was the director of the Cedar Springs Development Company. The overall development, roughly square in shape, was southeast of Inwood between Maple and Cedar Springs. The developers donated land to the city for Cherrywood Park, at Cedar Springs and Hudnall. The first houses offered for sale were just southwest of it. The neighborhood was called Hedgerow Park and began selling in 1938. It was a planned development selling completed, architect-designed houses. It carefully adhered to the standards specified by the Federal Housing Administration in order to qualify for their loans, intended to spur residential construction as the Depression lingered.

ARLINGTON PARK ESTATES

This development was restricted to African American Dallasites. It opened in 1949 when Dallas still practiced segregation in schools, parks, and residential neighborhoods. Once freed, former slaves formed freedman's towns around the margins of Dallas, on land that was not particularly valued. The North Dallas Freedman Town, now the Uptown area, was a fully functioning community with stores, churches, and community organizations. Many of the small houses were rental units owned by white outsiders. In contrast, the tiny Fields community in Lake Highlands was on land purchased by the Fields brothers from their former enslavers, the Caruth Family. Wheatley Place in south Dallas was established in 1916 and promoted as a neighborhood available to African American purchasers seeking new houses with modern bungalow styling and amenities like city water connections. South Dallas contained many other African American communities of various types, interspersed with neighborhoods reserved for white occupants.

By the end of World War II, African American neighborhoods had been over-crowded for decades, with no new areas in which to expand. Starting in the 1920s, individual families tried moving beyond the borders and were met with resistance, sometimes violent. The influx of war industry workers to Dallas exacerbated crowding. In the 1950s, resistance included bombings of homes. To solve what was called the "negro housing problem," city officials worked with some leaders in the African American community to build new, segregated subdivisions. Many of those seeking new homes were professionals

Figure 18: This is a 1967 image of Cherrywood Park, with Cedar Springs Road to its right. The houses of the Hedgerow Park neighborhood are visible to the left of the park. Photograph by Squire Haskins. Courtesy of the Dallas Municipal Archives.

achieving middle-class status, who wanted a modern house with a yard, like most people wanted after World War II.

The answer for these home-seekers would be Arlington Park and Hamilton Park. Arlington Park was located on acreage between Harry Hines and the river, between Record Crossing Road and the Chicago and Rock Island Railroad. Developers were not rushing into lands so near the Trinity levees, even though in theory they were safe from flooding, and few people want to live near a railroad. Hamilton Park was built at what would become the corner of Central Expressway and Loop 635. It was so far north that nobody could imagine it ever being desirable land.[8]

In 1950, city council member Roland Pelt proposed an entire African American town to be built in the levees south of Harry Hines. It would include residential and commercial development, as well as full educational infrastructure. Though it sounded wonderful in many ways, it was also a plan to establish a bastion of continuing segregation. Pelt argued that the plan would be "the answer to Negro housing for at

---

8   The negotiations and activities that led to the creation of Hamilton Park were first examined by Jim Schutze in *The Accommodation: The Politics of Race in an American City*, (Secaucus, N.J.: Citadel Press, 1986). To learn more about Hamilton Park, see William H. Wilson, *Hamilton Park: A Planned Black Community in Dallas*, (Baltimore: The Johns Hopkins University Press, 1998). No similar study of Arlington Park has been published.

1957 Tornado

On April 2, 1957, a tornado took a 16-mile path of death and destruction from Oak Cliff, through West Dallas, across the Trinity River, and passing through the Love Field area before turning to the northwest and fading away. The tornado took its time and left its mark, lasting for forty-six minutes, and as reported in the following day's paper killing nine people, injuring 170, and causing $1,500,000 worth of damages.

The front page headline on the April 3, 1957, edition of *The Dallas Morning News* noted the devastation in Oak Cliff and Northwest Dallas; however, what the headline didn't capture was that the worst hit area was in the Arlington Park community around Record Crossing Road and Riverside Drive. Four people were killed in Arlington Park, and of those three were children from the same family.

Figures 19A and B: A tornado in 1957 damaged houses in the neighborhood and neighboring buildings. Courtesy of the Dallas Firefighters Museum.

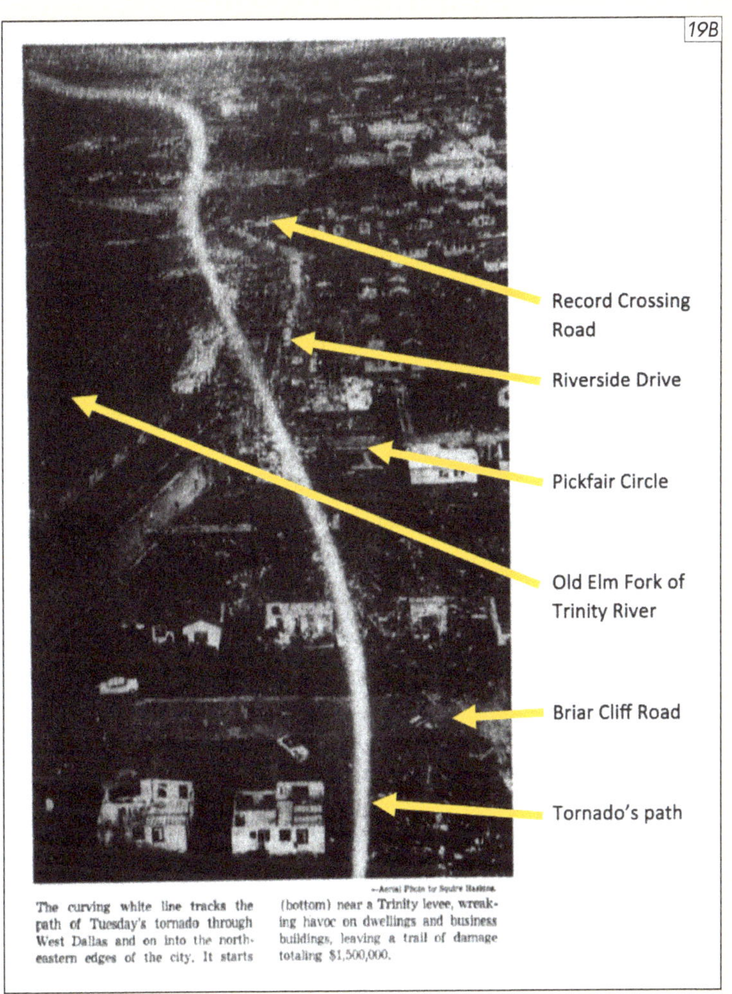

—Aerial Photo by Squire Haskins.

The curving white line tracks the path of Tuesday's tornado through West Dallas and on into the northeastern edges of the city. It starts (bottom) near a Trinity levee, wreaking havoc on dwellings and business buildings, leaving a trail of damage totaling $1,500,000.

This tornado was historic. Most of the rain from the storm had passed, so there was little to impede viewing of the tornado as it moved through urbanized areas of Dallas. At the time, it was the most photographed and filmed tornado in the nation. Even to this day, the April 2nd tornado claimed the most lives of any tornado to strike in the Dallas-Fort Worth area.

least fifteen to twenty years."[9] That grand plan was not completed, but a smaller part of the floodplain did become Arlington Park.

That period after World War II offered new hope for better housing for everyone. For veterans, cheap loans from the Federal Housing Administration (FHA) were an enticement to homeownership, though they rarely went to African American veterans. They were not generally available for old properties or those in racially mixed neighborhoods. Arlington Park was planned to be eligible for FHA loans, with houses that met guidelines and would have the required water, sewer, and gas service. It was also to have a park on the river for recreation and a school.

Not all of these promises were kept, at least not right away. Some streets remained unpaved, and the neighborhood had to fight for annexation into Dallas and to get trash and postal service. At first, land buyers could not find any construction companies willing to build houses for them, at any cost. Original home prices were $4,750 to $6,500.

The unexpected pace of postwar growth reached Arlington Park sooner than anyone had envisioned. With rising land values, residents faced a danger of being dispossesed of their homes for more expensive development. In 1961, residents resisted possible threats to the future of their houses: rezoning for apartments for commercial uses, as requested by developers. These proposed developments were in response to the needs of the hospitals that were creeping closer. The people of Arlington Park saw their best defense in keeping their single-family zoning.

In 1966, Trammel Crow himself voiced the developers' view — and verified the residents' fears. Representing investors holding land around the neighborhood, he discouraged the Dallas School Board from building a planned replacement for Arlington Park Elementary School. His argument was that investors were buying and holding so much land for redevelopment for commercial uses connected to the hospitals that there would soon be no residents to require a school. The existing residents did not agree. Their children's schooling became a focal point of their fight to keep and improve the community.

The continuing expansion of the Southwestern Medical School was particularly concerning in the next few years. In 1968, the Dallas

9   Lyle, Dorothea, "Pelt Recommends Site for Negro Community," in *The Dallas Morning News*, Feb. 26, 1950, p. 1.

Figure 20: In 1966 Arlington Park Elementary was still housed in this temporary building. Courtesy of the Dallas Public Library.

School Board seemed prepared to sell the elementary school's land to the Medical School if requested for expansion and began relocating students to other schools. Nearby schools with majority white student populations were passed over for that relocation, and the children sent further away to overcrowded African American schools. The city had begun a desegregation plan in 1961 but had made no real progress.

Arlington Park resident Sam Tasby played a leading role in bringing the school to Arlington Park, and later in Dallas' desegregation battle. The World War II veteran purchased his house when it was new and lived there until he was ninety. He had led the residents in demanding the creation of Arlington Park Elementary in 1957. After becoming the Arlington Park Community Learning Center, it was closed in 2012, along with ten other schools, for financial reasons. Neighborhood resident Carolyn Harrison later remembered, "When our school was closed, it took the heart out of Arlington Park Estates, and that was not good."

Though the school was a boon to the neighborhood, Tasby was soon disappointed by the inferior education his children received in a segregated school system. He became the lead plaintiff in the 1970 lawsuit that eventually commanded the desegregation of Dallas schools. When he filed his lawsuit in 1970, it had been sixteen years since the Supreme Court ruled that segregation was unconstitutional and provided unequal education. The lawsuit, Tasby v. Estes, dragged on for years with numerous injunctions, appeals, and court orders, any legal strategy that could delay resolution. In 1981, United States District Judge Barefoot Sanders, Jr. was assigned to the case, which had stalled as parties debated desegregation plans. He established a plan by official judgment, and the federal court maintained oversight of the plan's implementation until 2003.

The residents continue to honor the veterans who originally settled the neighborhood—both military veterans and those who were veterans of the fight to have their own community. In 2011, Tasby and eighteen other residents who achieved the age of ninety were honored at the "Kings and Queens Legends" party. Such long-term residents had come to the neighborhood seeking community and had built it with

Figure 21: Sam Tasby with his son Philip in their Arlington Park home, 1972. Courtesy of the Dallas Public Library.

institutions like the school and the Arlington Park Baptist Church. As the city crept closer, the security of that community was endangered.

Figure 22: A gathering in the Arlington Park home of Reverend Butler. Courtesy of the Dallas Public Library, Dallas History and Archives.

The varied people who have lived and worked in and around the Medical District are part of its history. Twenty-first century planning ideas evolved beyond the strict separation of uses that was promoted after World War II. Hospitals and nearby light industrial uses ceased to be seen as incompatible with housing and community retail. The sins of the past are now being recognized, as people learn about the evils of segregation. The surviving historic neighborhoods can continue as vital parts of the Medical District.

Figures 23 and 24: These two artworks were part of a 1993 commemoration of the community's history. The Community Legacy Tree (above) was installed in the Arlington Park Recreation Center and includes nameplates for honored residents. The artwork (right) was created by Freddie Gardner for the Arlington Park Community Reunion booklet. Both of these images and the map above are from a collection donated by Kathy Richey Farrington.

THE INSTITUTIONS
OF THE MEDICAL DISTRICT

Today's Southwestern Medical District is the end result of a struggle that began as soon as Dallas saw itself as a city. The early goal to provide Dallasites with medical care grew into a quest for Dallas to become a medical leader statewide and on the national scene. An early competitor in this race, as in so many others, was Houston, and there

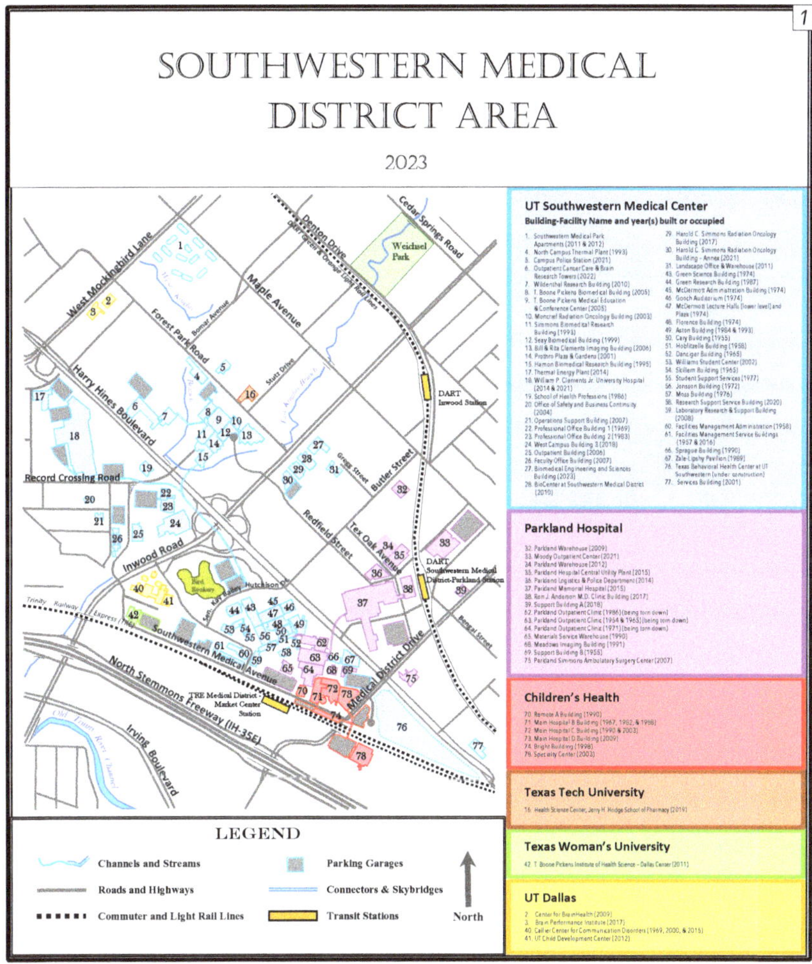

Figure 1: The institutions of the Southwestern Medical District, circa 2020. Courtesy of Robert Prejean.

remains no clear winner in that competition. The major occupants of the mature Medical District: University of Texas Southwestern Medical Center, Parkland Memorial Hospital, and then Children's Medical Center Dallas all grew from these early efforts.

SOUTHWESTERN MEDICAL:
THE FOUNDATION, THE SCHOOL, THE HOSPITAL

The legacy institutions of the Southwestern Medical Foundation give the District its current name. The Foundation began as an effort to establish medical training in early Dallas. The goal of physician training was one of the innovative elements the foundation brought to the ongoing development of a western Dallas hospital district. Expansion was made possible by the nature of post-World-War-II society. Science, expertise, research, and higher education were enjoying a period of popularity, as they had helped win the war. The economy was expected to grow, with rising standards of living and higher public expectations for resources, including healthcare.

Formal medical education is not nearly as old as one might think. Up to the latter 1800s, a man (almost always a man) was a doctor if he said he was a doctor. Training often involved working with experienced doctors and reading the available literature. Medical schools existed, Philadelphia had one by 1765, but they were not numerous, and not required. Frontier and recently frontier regions like Texas certainly lagged behind as the year 1900 approached.

The first significant attempt at a medical school in Dallas was the early Baylor Medical College. It was housed in a few rooms of a food-production complex owned by Dr. John Hughes south of downtown, and in the recently abandoned building of Temple Emanu-El. It was

Figure 2: Dr. Edward Cary in 1945 welcomes Fred Lange on the porch of a temporary office. Mr. Lange is arriving to take up his new role as Vice-President and Managing Director of the Southwestern Medical Foundation. Dr. Cary was the President of the foundation and the dean of the new school. News and Publications Collection, UT Southwestern Archives and Special Collections.

initially called the University of Dallas Medical Department, despite the lack of any actual University of Dallas. The desire to be linked to a larger educational institution became a theme in local medical education, as it could provide funding, legitimacy, and security.

At one point in those early years, Dallas had three nascent medical schools. The local medical community universally supported the educational ideal, but differences in philosophy, personality, and goals caused infighting and frequent changes of affiliation. Still, Dallas did begin to develop modest medical education through hospital practice. Baylor might have grown to be the first and only major medical school in Dallas, and the pioneer and namesake of the Medical District, but their goals clashed with those of city leaders in 1943. Baylor wanted city support for new facilities, but the city required them to loosen ties with Baptist leadership and be more non-sectarian. The medical school responded by moving to Houston. Thus, Houston won one battle in the long rivalry between the cities.[1]

Dr. Edward H. Cary offered Dallas its own solution. He had been associated with Baylor for over twenty years, but not without conflict. He sided with the non-sectarians. He did not follow Baylor to Houston. He did help a new organization step right into the place Baylor had planned and then abandoned: a new facility near the second location for Parkland Hospital and a new mutual arrangement of hospital training for medical students. Cary, an earnest man of science, also had connections among Dallas' political and business elite. The Southwestern Medical Foundation could not have built and defined a new medical district northwest of downtown without their support. Cary had experience at building facilities and challenging existing standards. In 1923, he gathered investors to erect the Medical Arts Building at St. Paul and Pacific. At eighteen stories tall, it was quite visible in a still mostly short city. It housed medical offices and hospital facilities, and Cary hoped it would foster cooperation among the divided local medical community. It did. He became a local and national leader in medical organizations. In 1939, he led the incorporation of the Southwestern Medical Foundation, with a board of directors full of noted Dallas leaders, all with many resources.

---

1 For the complete story of the creation of the school, see John S. Chapman, *The University of Texas Southwestern Medical School: Medical Education in Dallas 1900–1975*, (Dallas: Southern Methodist University Press, 1976).

One of those was Karl Hoblitzelle. He built the successful Interstate Theater Company, providing entertainment throughout Texas and neighboring states. He was also a real estate investor. One of his many philanthropic donations to the Foundation was seventy-six acres of land in 1945. It was the tract at the south side of Harry Hines at Inwood. That gift ensured that the geographic growth of post-war medical infrastructure in Dallas would be northwest of downtown.

Mr. Hoblitzelle worked closely with Dr. Cary from the inception of the school and was its co-founder. He remained a major donor as well as being actively involved in leadership on the board. His wife, Esther, was a collector of fine and decorative arts, and when she died in 1943, she left that collection to the Hoblitzelle Foundation, which the couple founded the year before. Its massive and wide-ranging giving includes extensive help to medical organizations, as well as to art, history, and the indigent. On his giving, Mr. Hoblitzelle once stated, "I am inclined to lean toward programs which in general involve the discovery, transmission, and extension of facts, thoughts, ideals and ideas."[2] At his death in 1967, he left an estate valued around $17 million to the foundation.

Dr. Cary's wide network of influential contacts also helped him gain another mark of favor for the college-official designation as the second medical college in the University of Texas system in 1949. This raised prestige and lowered tuition. The college's relationship with UT leadership was not always smooth, but it remained beneficial.

The college's building program was slow to start and slow to finish, even as the war ended and returning soldiers wished to pursue medical training en masse. Portable structures for labs and classrooms may well have reminded them of their military accommodations. The class that entered in 1949 included a significant student from the Medical District. Onesimo Hernández was a child of Little Mexico. His family moved there after they spent his first years laboring in rural agricultural areas. He graduated from Crozier Technical High School, the only public option available for Mexican American children. In 1943, he left for military flight training. The war ended before he graduated. Seeing limited opportunities as a civilian pilot, he explored other career options.

---

2   McCormick, Harry, "Hoblitzelle Gifts Total $4,000,000," in *The Dallas Morning News*, June 19, 1960, p. 1.

Figure 3: The first Southwestern Medical School buildings were located near the original site of Parkland Hospital on Maple Avenue. They were made of plywood. The sign states that these are "temporary quarters." Courtesy of UTSW.

Figure 4: 'Karl Hoblitzelle: Dallas' Theater Magnate'. D Magazine. Hoblitzelle and his wife helped establish the Hoblitzelle Foundation in 1942. Since its founding, the foundation has given more than $250 million to various causes around Dallas, including more than 3,400 grants and more than 42 grants of more than $1 million. Causes have ranged from medical and social services to education and the arts. [https://www.dmagazine.com/publications/d-ceo/2023/january-february/karl-hoblitzelle-was-dallas-theater-magnate/]

He still vividly remembered his mother's tragic death when he was thirteen, and what it taught him about the consequences of inadequate medical care for the people of Little Mexico. As she bled to death from a miscarriage, the staff at Parkland Hospital failed to help her. He suspected this was due to her race, though he later learned through experience that the pace of work at a public hospital could lead to such tragedies.[3] This may have been on his mind as he chose to pursue a medical career and joined other veterans in the temporary structures of the Southwestern Medical School. His specialty would be surgery.

Figure 5: Yearbook photo of Onesimo Hernández, member of the incoming freshman class of 1949 at UT Southwestern. Hernández wore a suitably serious expression as he embarked on a lifetime of medical accomplishments. Image Courtesy of UT Southwestern.

He graduated near the top of his class and interned at Parkland. When he was ready to join a hospital staff as a full-fledged surgeon, both Methodist and Baylor hospitals rejected him. St. Paul Hospital accepted him, and he became the first physician of Mexican descent on their staff.

That institution began as St. Paul's Sanitarium in east Dallas, far from today's Medical District. It started, as so many did, in a modest building, soon replaced. The new building erected in 1895 was a romantic structure at the corner of Bryan and Hall streets. The modern facilities included one of the first Dallas installations of hot and cold running water.

In the early 1900s, it also served the nascent cause of medical education in Dallas, allied with the SMU Medical Department. Primacy in local medical education had arguably been won by the Southwestern Medical School by the 1950s, just as the inadequacies of St. Paul's aging facilities were proving untenable. In 1958, the decision was made to relocate to the growing Medical District, where Dallas' medical future seemed focused. The hospital also dropped an "s" in their name to become St. Paul Hospital. After five years of fundraising and

---

3   See Jane Guzman, "Opening Doors: Dr. Onesimo Hernández: Mexican American Pioneer," in *Legacies: A History Journal for Dallas and North Central Texas*, 5:1, Spring, 1993, pp. 38-42.

Figure 6: This watercolor portrait of Dr. Hernández was painted by David Chapa in 1996. Courtesy of Old Red.

construction, the new building opened. It was just across Inwood from the growing Southwestern facilities.

Even as their original building aged, St. Paul's staff was socially innovative. In 1954, five African American physicians joined the staff, though the hospital itself was not fully integrated until 1959. In a departure from expectations of the time, their nursing school graduated twenty-four male nurses before ending the admittance of male students in 1958. Working with their founders and constant partners, the nuns of the Sisters of Charity, the hospital opened the Marillac Clinic in 1928 to serve the residents of Little Mexico. Services included night classes in language and citizenship. The hospital's acceptance of Dr. Hernández was part of this pattern of inclusion.

His work at the hospital and in private practice could have been enough of a contribution, but Dr. Hernández went beyond those accomplishments: politics and volunteering. He failed to win political office in 1960 but became an influencer when invited to join the usually all-white Citizens Charter Association. The candidates they promoted for city office regularly won and had been doing so for forty years when they tried to superficially integrate their membership and candidate list in the 1960s. Dr. Hernández realized they considered him a "token," but he did use the experience to learn how to win in Dallas politics and to help other candidates gain office.

In his volunteer efforts, he worked with Southwestern Medical School to increase the number of Hispanic students. He served on boards for educational, medical, and charitable organizations. In 2016, his ground-breaking career and years of work for the people of Dallas County was officially recognized by the Dallas County Commissioners Court. The new medical facility for the county jail was named for Dr. Hernández and for Jesse Everett Gill, the first African American Dallas deputy sheriff. Onesimo Hernández Elementary School at 5555 Maple Avenue is another way the city has honored this child of Little Mexico.

Figure 7: The completed medical school building with Parkland behind it, as they appeared in 1955. Courtesy of Parkland.

As he began his career, his alma mater was also moving forward. In 1952, noted Dallas architect Mark Lemmon, responsible for many of the buildings at SMU, drew plans for a new medical school structure. His beautiful design could not be built for the money the college regents had available. Fundraising began, including among the college's first graduated classes, now alumni. The construction was only made possible by appropriations at the state level, for which Foundation president Dr. George M. Aagaard had to fight. Having won the battle in exhaustion, he resigned and left town. That first permanent building was completed and put into use in 1954. Originally called the Basic Science Hall, it was renamed after Dr. Cary in 1960, an honor he well deserved. The need for space continued to grow, as did the infrastructure to meet those needs.

Parkland and the Southwestern Medical College were symbiotic partners, each relying on the other. Parkland provided patients to give students practical experience and the College provided affordable medical practitioners. As both campuses grew, their buildings became intertwined on their shared land. Buildings filled in the empty spaces and grew taller. By 1989, James W. Aston Ambulatory Care Center,

Sprague, and Zale Lipshy facilities, affiliated with the school, flanked Parkland's building. Even with floors at different heights, they were all connected for convenience. It became difficult to distinguish them. One partner had physically engulfed the other.

The size of the faculty and the student body expanded along with the buildings. At the end of the 1950s, there were 100 full-time faculty members, 400 students, and 100 clinical residents. In the 1970s, the school added 1.5 million square feet of construction. The faculty grew to 500, teaching 800 medical students and 400 students in training programs in allied health sciences and graduate biomedical research. Through the 1980s, they acquired land and their building program made major incursions into the lands to the north and northwest. With the West Campus, the North Campus, and the South Campus, they fully occupy three quadrants of the Harry Hines and Inwood intersection and have a toehold in the fourth, east of Inwood.

The college was expanding its operations to research and starting more teaching hospitals. A new name, The University of Texas Southwestern Medical Center at Dallas, reflected the new, multi-component organization. In 1985, Drs. Joseph L. Goldstein and

Figure 8: Harry Hines stretches from the front of this bird's eye view toward downtown Dallas. The intersection with the cloverleaf at the center is where Inwood crosses. The O'Donnell Grove of trees, in the lower left quadrant of that intersection, was planted at the North Campus in 2000. It officially honors longtime supporters Edith J. and Peter O'Donnell, but it can also be seen as a tribute to the original natural occupants of the area and to the health benefits of trees. Courtesy of UTSW.

Michael S. Brown, both of the Health Science Center, were awarded the Nobel Prize in Physiology or Medicine for their discoveries about the metabolism of cholesterol. It was the first such honor awarded in Texas. The Nobel committee again recognized the Center's work in 1988. Dr. Johann Deisenhofer shared the Nobel Prize in Chemistry. He used an x-ray technique called crystallography to map the structure of a protein involved in photosynthesis. Yet again in 1994, Dr. Alfred Gilman brought Nobel recognition to the Center for his work with "G proteins," which help cells communicate with each other.

Such recognition doubtless helped the Center's successful fundraising in the 1980s and 1990s. High-profile donors such as Ross Perot funded new programs and the school was able to increase financial support for promising students. Donation continued into the twenty-first century with major gifts from the T. Boone Pickens Foundation, Annette and Harold Simmons, and former Texas Governor Bill Clements.

In 2011, the organization removed "in Dallas" from their name and became The University of Texas Southwestern Medical Center. They won another Nobel Prize and started construction of the William P. Clements, Jr. University Hospital further to the northwest than the Medical District had previously reached. Their renown was such

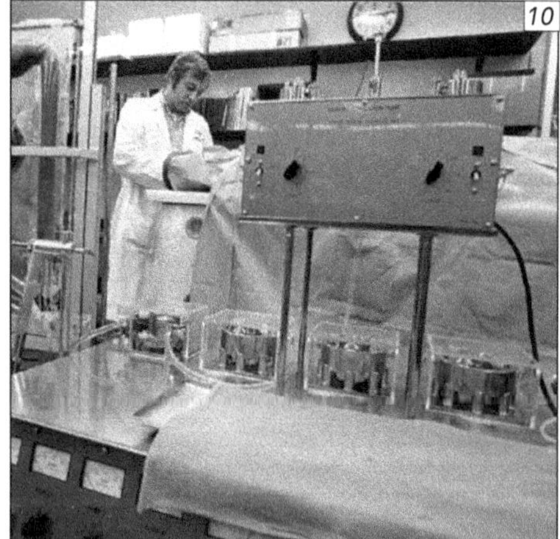

Figure 9: This microbe containment box protected people as they worked with dangerous contagions. Here research assistant Craig Wallace of the Microbiology Department works with test tubes inside of it, circa 1954. Figure 10: This heart-lung machine pumped blood and oxygen to maintain proper levels in a patient. Maintaining peak performance required the careful attention of a trained technician called a "perfusionist." Jack S. "Stan" Fennig is pictured working on the machine circa 1976. Source UTSW Hospital.

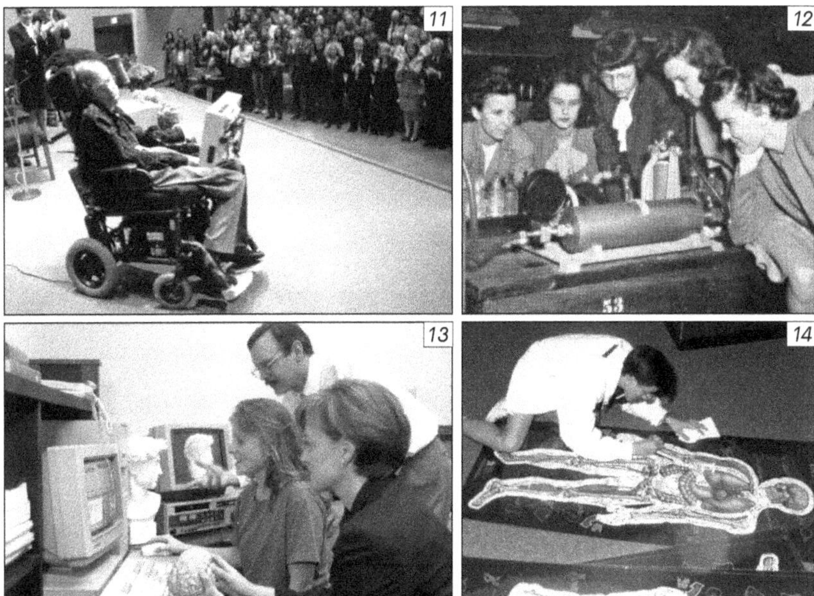

Figure 11: Stephen Hawking visited the school in 1998 to join a panel discussing the prevention and treatment of amyotrophic lateral sclerosis, ALS. Figure 12: These five women were part of the freshman class of 1946. Female students were still so rare as to merit this special photograph documenting their presence. Figures 13 and 14: Students studying medical illustration (above) learn to produce detailed instructional materials, such as the "body maze" (bottom right) that a future doctor is carefully studying. Source UTSW Hospital.

that everybody understood that they were in Dallas—they no longer needed it in their name. The original plan of the Southwestern Medical Foundation back in 1943 to tie medical education to hospitals, in close proximity, helped every occupant of the Medical District thrive.

THE CREATION OF PARKLAND AND WOODLAWN HOSPITALS

Physicians were valued newcomers on the frontier, where healthcare was sometimes in short supply. That situation improved as Dallas became more urbanized, and qualified physicians worked with city leaders to provide health services to all citizens, including those who could not pay. Beginning in 1874, the city maintained a City Hospital downtown, a government-funded facility for treating the indigent. It was manned by the City Physician. In the early years, this contract job was awarded to the lowest bidder, and the facilities were inadequate. A qualified candidate, Dr. Carter, held the new position of Health

Dallas' Medical Center at Maple and Oak Lawn Avenues

by Robert Prejean

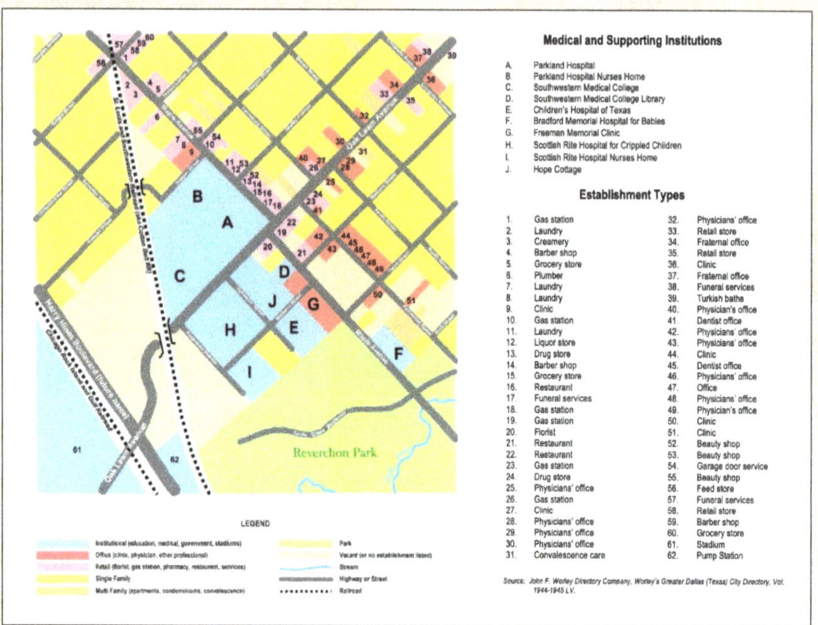

Before today's Southwestern Medical District along Harry Hines Boulevard, Dallas' earlier medical center was located around the intersection of Maple and Oak Lawn Avenues. The three member institutions that make up the Southwestern Medical District can trace much of their early beginnings around this intersection. It started in 1890. Dallas had become the largest city in Texas; however, public health facilities in Dallas were limited and considered deplorable. In 1893, Dallas city voters approved $40,000 to build a new city hospital on 14+ acres of picturesque, city-owned park space out in the country and far from the city. The next year the city hospital opened and was referred to as Parkland Hospital. Decades later, Dallas County would assume ownership and oversight of Parkland Hospital.

As the city expanded and overtook the city hospital, new residential subdivisions were built defined by a street grid walkable to transit, services, restaurants, and jobs. On the minor side streets, most of the housing was single family, but closer to Maple and Oak Lawn Avenues, apartments would be intermixed with single family housing and clinics. The automobile had established its dominance as gas stations occupied key corners, but within an easy walk were florists, pharmacies, barber and beauty shops, small grocers, and restaurants, including several barbecue shops, serving nearby residents, visitors, and hospital employees. Reverchon Park and Turtle Creek were in proximity to the medical center.

Parkland Hospital attracted both adult and pediatric medical facilities, clinics, doctors' offices, support services, and research college that decades later evolved into UT Southwestern Medical Center. Today's Children's Health System of Texas is the merging of various pediatric clinics and hospitals located in this medical center, including the Bradford Memorial Hospital for Babies, Freeman Memorial Clinic, and Texas Children's Hospital. Along with the institutions that would later become Children's Health were Hope Cottage, and Scottish Rite Hospital for Crippled Children, today's Texas Scottish Rite Hospital for Children that is still located at this intersection. This cluster of medical-related establishments around the intersection of Maple and Oak Lawn Avenues was the major medical center in Dallas before 1954 when Parkland Hospital moved to its new building on the outskirts of Harry Hines Boulevard.

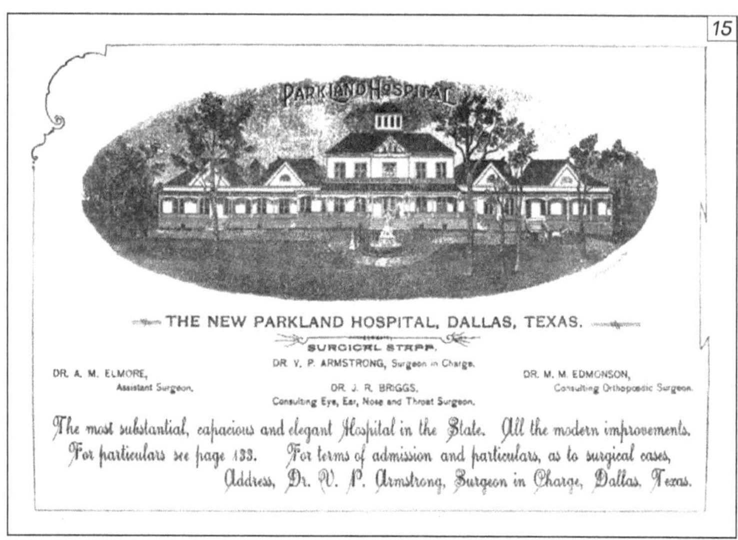

Figure 15: This advertisement for the new hospital depicts its first building and lists the medical staff available there. It was published in 1894. Courtesy of Parkland.

Officer when the city expanded the downtown facility in 1886. The new expansion allowed Dallas to boast that no city had a "better eleemosynary (charitable) institution." Its lack of vermin was noted, along with adequate food and abundant light to aid recovery. Dr. Carter invited citizens to come see it.[4]

One year later, he complained that it was overcrowded.[5] With a capacity of twelve patients, he was treating twenty-seven. It was expanded via the addition of a relocated old schoolhouse, while a new building was planned. This pattern would be repeated. Every hospital and quarantine or convalescent facility built by the city and county outgrew its facility sooner than expected.

That same year, 1887, the mayor of Dallas announced the acquisition of forty-five acres of new parkland north of the water reservoir. The reservoir was located about where Oak Lawn Avenue currently meets Interstate 35E. City officials named it North Dallas Park and suggested many other possible uses including hospitals or a reform home for boys. Such institutions were not wanted near thriving city neighborhoods. While these uses were initially dismissed for an area prone to flooding, they did come to pass in the eventual Medical District.

---

4   "The City Hospital," in *The Dallas Morning News*, Aug. 5, 1886, p. 5.
5   "The City Hospital," in *The Dallas Morning News*, Dec. 26, 1987, p. 5.

Figures 16 and 17: Original wooden Parkland Hospital on Oak Lawn Avenue as it appeared when new. Its most welcoming feature was the side open porch. Courtesy of the Dallas Public Library. The hospital acquired its first horse-drawn ambulance in 1894. This one was in service when the photograph was taken in 1911. Later, rubber tires were added to increase patient comfort. Dr. John Hicks Florence and family are pictured with nurses demonstrating the use of a stretcher. Courtesy of Historic Mesquite, Inc.

The city never did anything to develop North Dallas Park. In 1893, sixty-five acres of the unused parkland was dedicated to new city hospital facilities, eventually leading to the obvious name: Parkland Hospital. A grove of trees, including Pin Oaks, has been retained to this day on the grounds, recalling the potential for a wooded park and the earlier wild landscape.

The first buildings were one large and two smaller wooden structures. Many city hospital facilities remained downtown, including an emergency center in the basement of City Hall. An ongoing argument among medical experts and city officials debated if the next improved iteration should remain downtown for convenience. A plague of meningitis in 1911 settled the issue. It was decided that all functions of the perpetually pathetic city hospital should move away from downtown and take the potential for contagion with them.

Planning began for the first significant structure. It remains extant and is protected for the future as an official City of Dallas Historic Landmark. Local architects Hubbell & Green designed the two-story masonry building. It was 145 feet wide and 124 feet deep, in the fashionable Colonial Revival style, which was thought to give an air of permanence and competence. The cornerstone was laid in 1913. When completed one year later, it represented the latest in hospital design, the pavilion concept. To admit maximum light and air and allow the separation of patient areas, long, thin wings of rooms were built instead of a massive, centralized building. It was truly something to be proud of.

In 1915, that new building was "absolutely inadequate for the demands upon it," and so began a pattern of expansion, modernization, and obsolescence.[6] All additions were architecturally compatible with the original structure and continued the pattern of wings with many windows. A housing structure for nurses was added in 1921. The facility grew and changed for forty years until it was determined that it could not be improved enough to catch up with its growing responsibilities, and a new facility must be constructed.

Within the first two years of operation, x-ray and pathology laboratories were added. A previously unplanned basement was excavated under the main building. It was used as a segregated space to treat people of color. Provision had not originally been made for them in the

---

6   "Better Facilities for City Hospital," in *The Dallas Morning News*, July 7, 1915, p. 7.

Figure 18: This 1940 image shows the center columned portico, one of the original wings and the outer wing, added in 1921. Courtesy of the Dallas Public Library.

new hospital. As a county facility, it did follow generally accepted social ideas of separating people by race. However, Parkland was a bit more progressive when it hired its first African American nurse in 1937. Thirty-five-year-old Ollie Lee Mason went on to serve as a city public health nurse and worked for the Peace Corps. Her father, Dr. W. R. McMillan, owned and operated the McMillan Sanitarium until 1941. Such private facilities answered the medical needs of African Americans during segregation. His example doubtless inspired his daughter's interest in medicine.

The original Parkland Hospital established a precedent that followed it to its second location in the Medical District: the convenient grouping of medical facilities. *The Dallas Morning News* termed this grouping "hospital row" in 1926. There were so many medical options in the area that the newspaper asked, "If anyone should get hurt in the Parkland Hospital row, where will he be treated?"[7] Other hospital facilities located near the Oak Lawn facility, as did physicians' offices and medical suppliers. Though the site was originally chosen for isolation, easy access and the residential growth along Oak Lawn soon made it a more urban location.

The county had other public health needs to address. By the 1880s, it became common practice in public health to establish a hospital for those with contagious diseases out in the countryside, far from everyone else. In 1886, Dallas faced a smallpox epidemic. The City Hospital was also seeing indigent patients with Dengue Fever and

---

7   "They Also Serve," in *The Dallas Morning News*, Jan. 18, 1926.

Yellow Fever. Smallpox was a fearsome disease because it was highly contagious. It had about a thirty percent death rate, with children and older people more likely to survive, but marked by scars. In the late 1700s, it was the first disease for which inoculation was practiced. Understandably, the idea of purposely infecting someone with a disease to keep them from getting sick seemed suspicious and was slow to catch on, until people saw that it worked. Smallpox remained a scourge until 1980, when it was declared eradicated from the Earth.

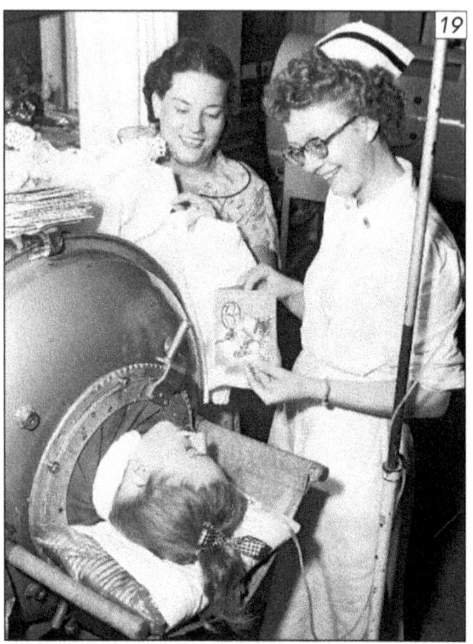

Figure 19: In July of 1952, the Oak Lawn facility was aging, yet still helping patients. Patient Mary Kate Sides needed an iron lung to help her breathe. In this image, her mother and nurse Betty Otto try to make her sixteenth birthday as happy as possible. Courtesy of the Dallas Public Library, Dallas History and Archives.

In response to the immediate danger, in 1886 the city of Dallas joined with the county to create a public hospital located in an isolated area beyond the city limits. The spot that qualified was in the Medical District, a forty-four-acre triangle of rural land within potential flooding distance of the Trinity. It was at the edge of the small Cedar Springs Lake, no longer visible, but located at the later southern corner of the intersection of Harry Hines and Medical District Drive. The isolated site was three miles from the city, a half a mile from the nearest house, and safely distant from the road. Initially named Suburban Hospital, the original building cost $845 and was built in twelve days.

By 1907, the aging structure was in poor condition and city officials called it an embarrassment to such a large and rich city. As repairs were completed, the name was changed from Suburban Hospital to Union Hospital. The official name change had no effect of the common use of the term "pest house." That name appears in official records and the newspaper. Suburban Hospital had been a useful name to reassure everybody it was safely far away. Union Hospital was a

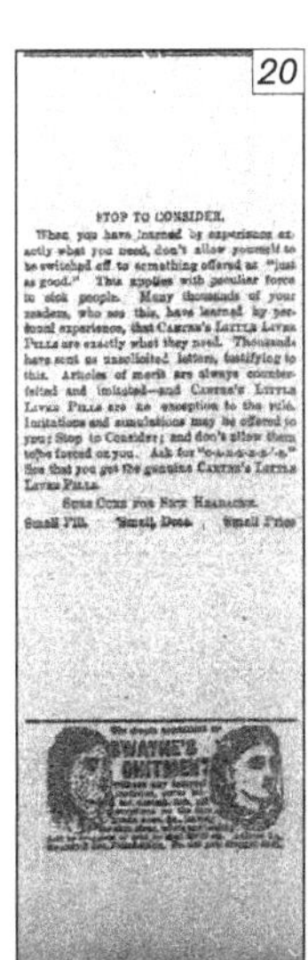

Figure 20: Physicians in private practice, such as Dr. J. R. Briggs, advertised their official status with Parkland. It served as recognition of their abilities and generosity in sharing their talents with needy patients. This advertisement was published in 1894. Courtesy of *The Dallas Morning News.*

neutral name, as the facility became a general house for the isolation of infectious diseases, not just for indigent people. Pest house was the most truthful name. It was a place of contagion and possible death that inspired fear.

In Dallas, as in other places, a victim of smallpox was immediately quarantined. The victim could choose to remain at home, but the whole family would be locked in for weeks with a sign posted outside that caused embarrassment and lasting ostracism.

Victims often chose the pest house instead, as the lesser of two evils. Members of the public understood the purpose of the pest house, probably approved of it as a protection for the city, and hoped to never actually enter its walls.

Another health problem plaguing the city during the hospital row era was tuberculosis. Tuberculosis, often called consumption, has existed in humans since ancient times. It is contagious, and the way it invades the lungs can cause constant coughing, sometimes bloody. Patients can become weak and pale. Some might recover, most did not. Many people were familiar with its effect on victims and risk of transmission, so it inspired fear. It remained a major threat until the 1940s, when over half a century of research began to produce viable cures.

The city addressed that need with Woodlawn Hospital, opened in 1913 to "admit as patients only those who are indigent and who are bona fide residents of the city or county of Dallas."[8] The County Medical Association recommended the name to the City Council. It was a joint city-county government endeavor located on twenty acres of land, the same plot as the then extant Union Hospital. The building originally cost $83,000.

Woodlawn Hospital was presented as both a point of humanitarian pride for the people of Dallas, and a matter of public

Figures 21 and 22: Both the front (top) and rear (bottom) of Union Hospital presented a domestic appearance, which hopefully offered some reassurance to arriving patients. Both courtesy of the Dallas Public Library.

safety. The health of the non-infected was protected by keeping all of the infected people isolated in hospitals until they recovered. In the period known as the Progressive Era (1890s to 1920s), some people promoted the need for society to help the impoverished and sick through institutions and programs. Others worried this would lead to dependence and lack of motivation. Providing a hospital for poor victims of tuberculosis was easy to paint as good for everybody in the city.

The 1913 building conformed to the standards of the time. Light and fresh air were thought key to helping the infected lungs heal. So, the hospital had large, high-ceilinged rooms with many windows, and over 200 feet of long, covered porches where patients could be wheeled to take the air.

In November 1947, Dr. Matthew J. Noon resigned from his position as director of the hospital in protest of maintenance cuts for the facility. In was becoming a miserable place for the sick. After the completion of the second Parkland, Woodlawn moved into the Old Parkland facility, and it was renovated. In 1956, Irving carpenter Ray

---

8   "Woodlawn Hospital is Formally Opened," in *The Dallas Morning News*, July 20, 1913, p. 1.

Figure 23: This photograph of the aging entry gates and buildings of Woodlawn appeared in the Parkland School of Nursing Yearbook in 1951. Courtesy of UTSW.

G. Shuler praised the facilities after staying there for nine months. "Woodlawn has a nice recreation hall, TV, dominoes, cards, movies every week. I got where I liked it—almost didn't want to go home."[9] Note that while television was becoming very popular in the 1950s, not every family could afford to own one right away.

Figure 24: Woodlawn Hospital stretched across the open land, with its own water tower. Courtesy of the Dallas Public Library.

The hospital was a frequent recipient of charitable efforts by Dallas groups. Celebrities might also be encouraged to help the patients by visiting. In June 1956, Leo Durocher was in town and sent out to Woodlawn. Patients who were baseball fans were doubtless excited, but patient June Stevens was much more interested in presenting him with a gift of embroidered pillowcases for his wife.[10]

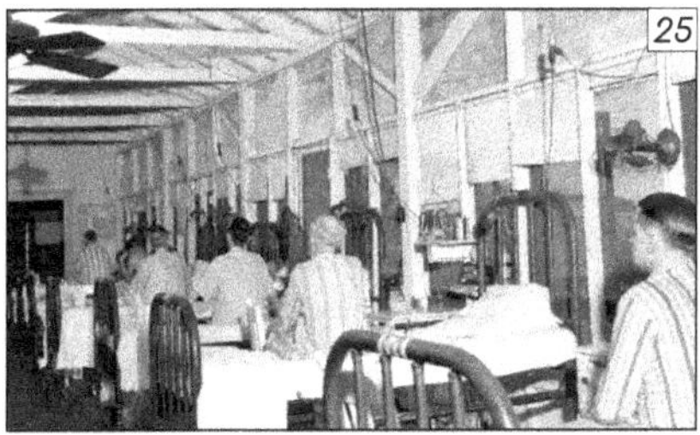

Figures 25 and 26: Image of the interior of Woodlawn Hospital. A patient ward. Telephone being used by a patient wearing a protective mask. Courtesy of the Dallas Public Library.

9 "Ex-TB Patients Tell of Hospitals," in *The Dallas Morning News*, Jan. 29, 1956, p. 12.

10 "TB Patients Give Durocher Present to Take to Laraine," in *The Dallas Morning News*, June 8, 1956, p. 6.

New ideas in public health fueled a county-wide tuberculosis eradication plan, operated by experts in an office in the basement of Woodlawn. The plan was to track and test every current or former TB sufferer in the county, and all of their family and contacts, in order to find and treat all active cases. It was thought that "lost" cases, those not identified, were a dangerous source of contagion.

As testing and eventual inoculations made housing tuberculosis patients a shrinking need, Woodlawn took on the care of patients with other health issues. From 1960 onward, these included general convalescents, the aged, alcoholics, the hearing impaired, and obesity patients. Woodlawn was closed and its operations moved to Parkland in 1974. Serious financial issues faced by the county hospital system primarily caused the change. Dr. Charles Sprague expressed concern about the dangers of integrating tuberculosis treatment in a facility with other patients.

In late 1975 and early 1976, Dallas County Commissioners proposed converting Woodlawn into a minimum-security prison, to alleviate crowding elsewhere. Renovations were begun. Neighbors

Figures 27 through 29: The original site of Parkland Hospital and its buildings languished without care after the county discontinued use of the site. When photographed by Robert Prejean in 2006, the landmark displayed crumbling stucco, broken and boarded windows, graffiti, and trash stored on the upper balcony. Note there were not even any posted "No Trespassing" signs to protect from vandalism. The site was saved by rehabilitation for office uses and became an official historic landmark for the city.

were concerned about the negative effect on the redevelopment and stabilization of Oak Lawn and opposed the plan. A lawsuit ended in late 1976, with a jury finding that the jail would not adversely affect nearby homes and businesses. Over the next twenty years, the neighborhood did revitalize, despite the presence of the prison.

By the time the value of the site was recognized as an important artifact of Dallas medical history in the mid-1980s, it was mostly known as Woodlawn, and the public had to be reminded of its first history as Parkland Hospital. It became better known as "Old Parkland" after 2006, when Harlan Crow purchased it and began restoring it as an office complex.

PARKLAND HOSPITAL ON HARRY HINES BOULEVARD

Parkland opened at its new location on Harry Hines in 1954. It also began with one large, impressive structure that promised to meet all potential needs. Then it was engulfed by an accretion of later additions and buildings in the inevitable process of growth and modernization. And like the first Parkland building before it, it was abandoned for a later facility that provided space and features that were unimaginable as ground was broken for the thoroughly modern 1954 Parkland.

Figures 30 and 31: The original hospital building, now known as "Old Main," (top) and the Nurses' Quarters, (bottom), as restored for new uses. Courtesy of Old Parkland.

The plan began in 1945 with a request for county bond funding of $7,000. The original Parkland was operated by the combined efforts of the county and city of Dallas. The site on Harry Hines was available, accessible via the new highway, but not very close to residences. Some local industry owners objected to the location, foreseeing how it might change their future business.

From the beginning, the plans for the new facility were connected to the educational efforts of the Southwestern Medical Foundation. A hospital

Figure 32: Under the ownership of Harlan Crow, a grove of historic Post Oak trees like those that once grew wild on the land is maintained. Courtesy of Old Parkland.

in which to practice was seen as a necessary part of physician training. For this reason, foundation President Dr. Edward Cary was among those pleading for the bond funding. The voters approved the bond and planning began in August. The operations of the original Parkland, and of Woodlawn, were governed by the City-County Hospital Board, which would direct the new effort.

Unexpected increases in construction costs altered plans by early 1947. Massive post-war construction was occurring across the nation, because so little had taken place during the Depression and the war. Material and labor costs rose. The estimated cost for the hospital almost doubled. The hospital board delayed the start of construction to 1948 and hoped the new opening date would be in early 1950. Additional money could be sought from a new federal grant program for the construction of hospitals. Controversy over the wisdom of accepting federal funding and potential federal interference delayed action, so it was not until 1952 that the construction contract could be awarded.

The planned building was in the form of a wide "T", with the main façade on the top of the T and the rest as a wing behind. Overall height was eight stories, thirteen in the center. The squares formed by the T are filled in with shorter sections. It was designed by local architect Roscoe DeWitt. His earlier work, such as Woodrow Wilson

Figure 33: The official groundbreaking shovel struggles against the former farmland of the Medical District. Pictured are County Judge Lew Sterrett, left, A. R. Davis, center, and Mayor J. B. Adoue Jr., right. Courtesy of the Dallas Public Library.

High School and buildings at Southern Methodist University, used historic styles. For post-war buildings such as Parkland, he worked with Arch B. Swank, Jr. in the modern International Style. Clean white walls were gridded with windows. The hospital that was supposed to open by 1948 did not have its groundbreaking until May 1, 1952. City officials used a three-handled shovel to turn the first dirt.

The hospital design once again reflected the latest trends, though it may not seem so to modern eyes. Private or semi-private rooms replaced wards where contagion was common and privacy unavailable. Interior materials such as polished concrete block walls, tile flooring, and acoustic ceilings were modern surfaces that promoted easy sanitation and noise suppression. A newspaper photograph reveals a hallway that looks clean but not cheerful or bright. It was far better than the basement hallway of the older Parkland facility published beside it. That was crowded with staff and patients, with an overall dingy appearance.

Figure 34: Parkland Hospital on Harry Hines in 1954, before many subsequent additions. Courtesy of Parkland Hospital.

During planning and construction, the new hospital was called the uninspired but descriptive name "city-county hospital." Both the Dallas City Council and the County Commissioners Court approved a requested name change to Parkland Memorial Hospital. Alumni of the original Parkland wanted its name recognized and preserved, with that older building slated to become Woodlawn Hospital. In 1954, it was officially designated as a memorial to American "war dead," when it was discovered that the original hospital 1945 bond issue included that intent.

The end of World War II brought efforts across the nation to honor those who had served. On the site of Parkland, this was first done through trees. In 1944, Woodlawn Hospital was on that land. The Texas Highway Department and the Dallas Garden Club sponsored a living memorial effort, the planting of 825 Redbud trees. Families could purchase a tree to be planted along Harry Hines. An official record and a tag applied to the tree would name the honoree. By year's end, they had planted 1,185. Women were included in the list of honorees. A sign was posted about the meaning of the trees. In 1947, when the city incorporated the area, they were moved to the Lawther Drive entrance to White Rock Lake.

When Parkland opened in September 1954, patients were transferred to the new hospital in twenty-eight ambulances and expressed approval of the new facility. Newspaper photographs let readers see

Figure 35: The original building is at center, seen from the rear. Decades of growth surrounds it, both additions to the original structure and the buildings of other institutions. Courtesy of Parkland Hospital.

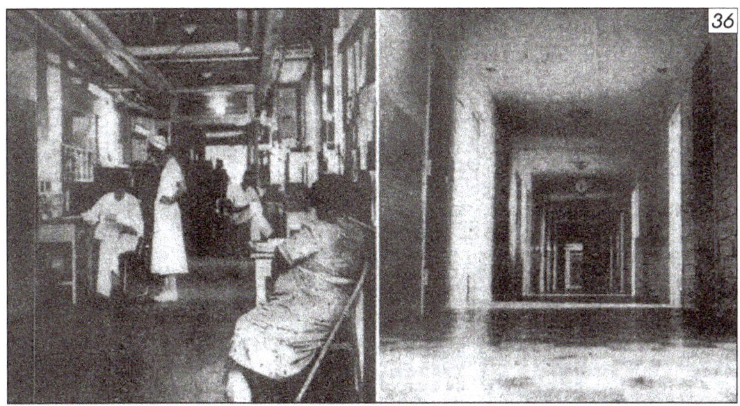

Figure 36: The Dallas Morning News *documented events as the staff and patients of Parkland Hospital on Oak Lawn prepared to move to the new building. They used these two images to illustrate the amazing difference between the two facilities. The basement hallway of the older building was used for patient care. It was dark, with exposed pipes above. Courtesy of* The Dallas Morning News.

amenities like the autoclave for sterilizing instruments, the giant soup pots for food preparation, and a still for producing distilled water. Happy nurses posed with smiling patients. They all clearly approved of the new facility. Dallas really had achieved a forward milestone in the development of its medical industry. A few weeks after the hospital opened, Dallas County voters overwhelmingly approved the creation of the Dallas County Hospital District to operate Parkland.

Figures 37 & 38: *Housing for nurses was first established at the Oak Lawn location in 1914 (#37), and then at the new hospital. Student nurses stand in front of their new quarters (#38). Courtesy of Parkland Hospital and the Dallas Public Library.*

The new hospital immediately began to pursue a course of medical innovation. In the first three years after opening, Parkland became the first civilian hospital in Texas to use an artificial kidney machine, soon followed by a dialysis unit. In 1955 and 1956, Parkland physicians performed the first Dallas corneal transplant and open-heart surgery. In 1961, they opened a sixteen-bed burn unit, among the nation's largest civilian facility. In 1962, the emergency room adopted a model system. It was divided into six treatment areas and sorted incoming patients using the nation's first nurse-directed triage system under Head Nurse Doris Nelson.

That emergency room would soon be the subject of national scrutiny. John F. Kennedy was rushed there on November 22, 1963, and Parkland physicians desperately tried to save his life. The gunshot wounds inflicted by assassin Lee Harvey Oswald defeated their best efforts. The national press carried images of the valiant work inside the hospital and the solemn people gathered outside.

Parkland hospital continued to embrace innovation. The installation of air conditioning in 1964 should not be overlooked for its beneficial effect for patients. In the 1960s, the medical staff also began publishing medical texts to share what they were learning from their innovative work.

The neonatal Intensive Care Unit opened in 1973, and a year later, the Epilepsy Treatment Center opened. In the 1970s Parkland also increased cooperation with UT Southwestern and the Dallas Fire Department's Emergency

Figure 39: The Dallas Morning News *celebrated the day patients moved to the new hospital, including Mrs. Jerry Snipes, suffering from a broken neck, transported wearing a brace and full makeup. Featured equipment included a still for water, giant soup pots in the kitchen, and an autoclave for sterilizing instruments. Courtesy of* The Dallas Morning News.

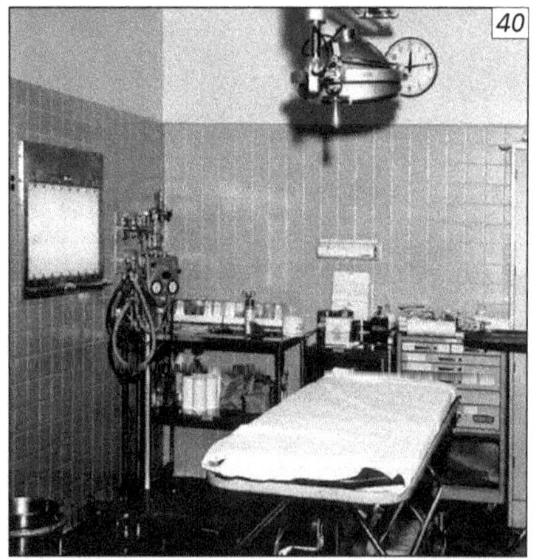

Figure 40: This is the emergency room where John F. Kennedy was treated. It was well-equipped for 1963. Courtesy of Parkland Hospital.

Medical Services. Parkland began the 1980s with voter approval of a new $80 million North Tower.

In the 1980s, Parkland was certified as the first Level One Trauma Center in Texas and opened the nation's first Pediatric Trauma Center. It became the first hospital in the Southwest to clinically use nuclear magnetic resonance imaging. They also fought inequities in the care of indigent patients. Parkland worked with officials to pass state and then national legislation to end the practice of "patient dumping." Patient dumping occurred when hospitals refused or transferred patients who could not pay for services but were in need of immediate medical help. Parkland continued to address difficult questions of equal treatment for the homeless past the year 2000. They also expanded operations into a network of smaller neighborhood facilities.

Figure 41: In 1975, Jerry and Debbie Davis were the proud parents of the first set of quintuplets born in Dallas. The babies faced some challenges, but the doctors and nurses at Parkland succeeded in bringing them to good health. Courtesy of UTSW. Figure 42: The ruins of the crashed plane at Dallas-Fort Worth International Airport in 1985 serve as evidence of the severity of this tragic event. Courtesy of Parkland.

On August 2, 1985, the hospital's trauma care facilities were tested when a Delta Airlines jet crashed at the Dallas-Fort Worth International Airport. A total of twenty-one survivors were taken to Parkland. As reported by the hospital's Chief Executive Officer, when staff saw the accident reported on the evening news right after it happened, they rushed to the hospital on their own initiative. "Within minutes, there were about fifty physicians waiting in the Emergency Room and nearly that many nursing personnel."[11]

The twenty-first century also brought the realization that once again, medical progress and the growing population of Dallas County

---

11   "Chief Executive Officer's Report, Aug. 27, 1985," Parkland Hospital Archives.

had rendered a once cutting-edge facility inadequate. The fourth Parkland building on the hospital's third site opened in 2015. As it rose, it dwarfed the 1954 building just across Harry Hines. From the day it was completed, the futuristic building was poised to continue Parkland Hospital's pursuit of innovation.

THE ORIGINS OF THE CHILDREN'S MEDICAL CENTER

The effort to provide Dallas children with healthcare began at Parkland Hospital's original location on Oak Lawn. The ideas that grew from the hospital's "Baby Camp," initially housed in a tent on the grounds, produced three early institutions: the Bradford Hospital, Richmond Freeman Clinic, and the Children's Hospital of Texas. Each began in the early 20th century and served underprivileged patients. They were the key progenitors of the modern Children's Medical Center Dallas.

The organizations' missions reflected the ideals of the Progressive Era of the 1890s to the 1920s. Many Progressive activists worked to improve conditions in cities by helping the poor, in something of a challenge to strict ideas of self-sufficiency. They used arguments that helping the poor improve their situation benefited everyone. They were particularly concerned about urban industrial workers. The most effective calls to action were for the benefit of children and the protection of

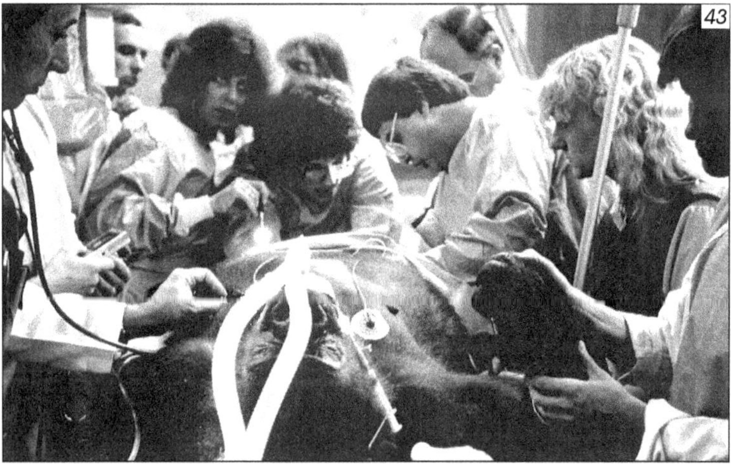

Figure 43: In 1985, the hospital performed an unusual examination. Denba resided at the Dallas Zoo, where she and her mate, Fubo, had been unsuccessful in producing any baby gorillas. Unfortunately, the examination found that Denba was unable to conceive. Courtesy of Parkland.

Figure 44: Like its 1954 predecessor, the latest Parkland Hospital building, to the right, exhibits the most modern style of its age. It is far larger than the original 1954 building, seen to the left, yet it will doubtless also grow too small as Dallas County's population and the needs of modern medicine expand. Courtesy of Parkland.

public health. If children could be provided with education, nutrition, and medical care, they would grow up to be more successful than their parents. Left without medical care, the poor could be the source of epidemics.

The efforts were often led by women of the middle and upper classes. In Dallas, one such effort provided clean, free milk from milk wagons to the mothers of small children. Dallas "club women," wives or daughters of successful men who joined clubs, also worked to provide playgrounds and battle child labor.

The woman who was instrumental in creating the first Dallas pediatric care facility was not a clubwoman but a nurse at the original Parkland Hospital: Miss May Forster Smith. The nursing profession often served Progressive ideas and helped provide careers for women. In 1913, Miss Smith accepted a new opportunity, and many Dallas children lived to adulthood because she did. Her supervisors asked her to take on the management of a new healthcare effort, a "baby camp" for the treatment of sick and malnourished babies. In later years, she modestly maintained that she was reluctant to accept such a task.[12]

However, she worked miracles in baby care, inspiring others to share her dream of building the baby camp into a great hospital, and beneath her outward modesty, she was a supremely capable and confident leader. In the first year of operation, her team treated 100 babies, many facing the common summer scourges of diarrhea and dehydration from dysentery.

The City Federation of Women's Clubs of Dallas supported the camp. Its members raised funds and gathered supplies. The facility was housed in tents on the grounds of Parkland, hence the term "camp." Local doctors volunteered their time. At first, the mothers were required to "surrender" the babies to the camp and stay away for the entire course of treatment. Generous though they might be, Progressive institutions often considered poorer people to be unskilled at properly caring for children. Organizers may have originally feared that parents would undo their good work in ignorance.

Figure 45: Nurses invoked the latest medical knowledge and practiced loving care to improve the health of babies. May Forster Smith resisted having her picture taken, so that few images are available. She can be seen here, on the far right. Courtesy of Children's Health Archives Center.

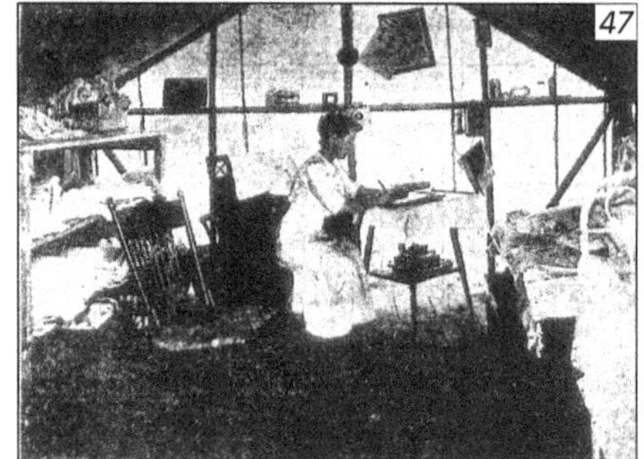

Figures 46 and 47: These tents among Parkland's wooded land on Oak Lawn initially housed the Baby Camp. Since the camp operated mostly in the summer and air conditioning was not yet available, the tents were a good option. Nurses even used a tent for their office. Both courtesy of Children's Health Archives Center.

---

12   See Jan Isbelle Fortune, "Memory of a Child Grown Up and Persistence of Her Nurse Story Behind Baby Hospital," in *The Dallas Morning News*, April 2, 1930, p. 28.

Later, parents were invited to see the babies and given training in proper care.

By 1915, the city and the Federation agreed to jointly provide a permanent hospital to replace the camp. Referred to as the Baby Camp Cottage, it was located across Oak Lawn from the original tent site. The city built it, the Federation maintained it, and fundraising efforts including a rummage sale equipped it.

Figure 48: Nurses used this homemade piece of equipment. The caption says it is the "Famous Baby Camp Incubator Which Has Saved Sixteen Little Lives." Courtesy of Children's Health Archives Center.

Figures 49 and 50: Two views of nurses outside of the building that replaced the tents. It still had many windows and screened openings to allow for fresh breezes. Both courtesy of Children's Health Archives Center.

Miss Smith continued to operate the new indoor baby camp. Over the next few years, she was visited by a little girl she had nursed to health in the past, who remained her loyal friend. Little Elizabeth Bradford would bring toys to the babies when she visited in her pony cart. As a young mother, she was killed in a car accident. Her father, who had earlier lost his wife as well, built Miss Smith the hospital of her dreams in their memory.

That generous donor was Thomas Leonard Bradford, a native of Louisiana. He opened a modest grocery in Oak Cliff in 1888, built it into a small chain, and went on to a career with Southwestern Life Insurance Company. He was elected to the first Dallas City Council in 1930, and his fellow council members elected him mayor. His son continued the family tradition of generosity for public health. In 1947, he donated the twenty-three room mansion his father built along the Cedar Springs Road to the nascent Pilot School for the Deaf. Deaf children learned in the house and played on its grounds until 1966. The school joined other medical institutions by moving to the Medical District. It became the Callier Center for

Figure 51: Local businessmen are delivering supplies to the Baby Camp, including live turkeys. The date of this event is not known. Courtesy of Children's Health Archives Center.

Communication Disorders located on Inwood Road. It is now part of the University of Texas at Dallas system.

The Bradford Memorial Hospital for Babies opened on New Year's Day, 1930. Construction delays had prevented the intended opening celebration, Thanksgiving dinner. Once again, it was furnished through volunteer fundraisers, including a card tournament. Mrs. Chrystine B. Carter, a local expert on interior décor, provided the decorations. The new hospital was a large stone building with new equipment, the fulfillment of May Smith's dreams.

Meanwhile, the Presbyterian Clinic, which would become the Richmond Freeman Clinic, also took their charitable ministrations directly to an impoverished area. Woodchuck Hill was across Oak Lawn from Old Parkland, the area later occupied by Reverchon Park. Many of its inhabitants were squatters with nowhere else to go.

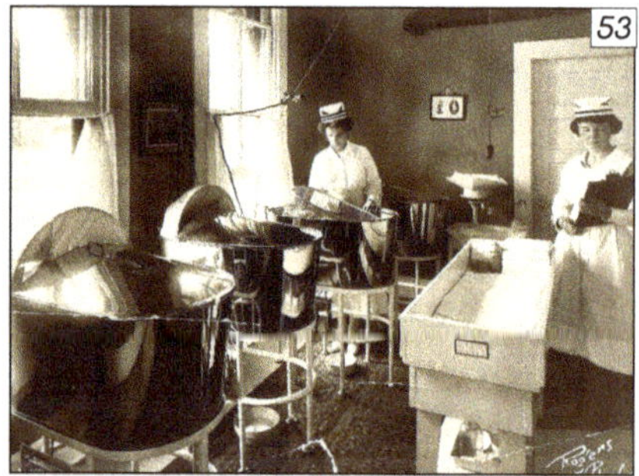

Figure 52: The large Bradford Hospital building of sturdy masonry construction and stylish design was quite an improvement over previous facilities. At the grand opening, those who had worked so hard to make the Bradford Memorial Hospital a reality posed with the reason for their hard work, a young patient in a crib. Courtesy of Children's Health Archives Center. Figure 53: The equipment at the new hospital was also impressive. These incubators, known as "Hess Beds," used hot water circulating between inner and outer metal baskets to warm babies. Courtesy of Children's Health Archives Center.

Figure 54: The hospital even had its own large laundry facility. Courtesy of Children's Health Archives Center. Figure 55: This circa 1910 image shows Woodchuck Hill as a gentle rise that attracted makeshift housing. Turtle Creek was nearby and could provide water. Courtesy of the Dallas Municipal Archives.

First Presbyterian Church originally opened their clinic in the church basement in 1921, with a kitchen table serving for a treatment surface. They had one doctor, two volunteers, and the church pastor for a staff. Within two years, they were serving too many patients for the basement to hold. In 1924, they also received a new hospital building created as a memorial. Percy Richmond Freeman Jr. died in 1920 at the age of twenty-seven. He was an up-and-coming local businessman. His distraught parents directed their sorrow to the cause of doing good in his honor. His mother did not survive to see the hospital become a reality, but his father spoke at the hospital opening of her devotion to the creation of the facility. The parents also insured that the institution would provide free care to all indigent patients without restrictions based on race, religion, or ethnicity.[13]

The new hospital was on Maple, in what is now the northern corner of Reverchon Park. After 1935, the institution used only the Richmond Freeman Clinic name. It was an education-oriented operation. Trained nurses and volunteers were sent out to the homes of the poor to examine children and teach parents about cleanliness, nutrition, and proper care. They witnessed the toll taken on children who had to work to help support the family. Newsboys, a perennial favorite target of Progressive reformers, might not be induced to give up their careers but were lured to the clinic for care. At the level of professional education, the clinic hosted the 1948 meeting of the Texas Pediatric Society on "medical problems of children ranging from blood disorders to bad behavior."[14]

---

13 Mamie Folsom Wynne, "Children of Needy Families Offered Treatment Without Cost at Presbyterian Clinic," in *The Dallas Morning News*, Dec. 19, 1926, p. 1.
14 Medical Problems of Children Due Airing at Clinic," in *The Dallas Morning News*, Oct. 10, 1948, p. 11.

These efforts were an impressive start, but the work needed to go further. In 1928, a group of local doctors proclaimed their intention to build a general hospital for children in Dallas, to fill a local, state, and southwest regional need. Organizers worked on winning the support of local government and citizens and on fundraising. The limitations of the Depression made the campaign languish. It was revived in 1938.

The same benefactor who made the Freeman clinic possible donated land right next to it, in proximity to Old Parkland and the Scottish Rite facility. The Depression was not over, but conditions were improving, and those dedicated to the cause of the hospital were able to renew fundraising. Construction of the Texas Children's Hospital, soon renamed Children's Hospital of Texas, began in 1939. The facility opened in 1940. It offered forty-seven beds, x-ray equipment, and a variety of specialists among its physicians.

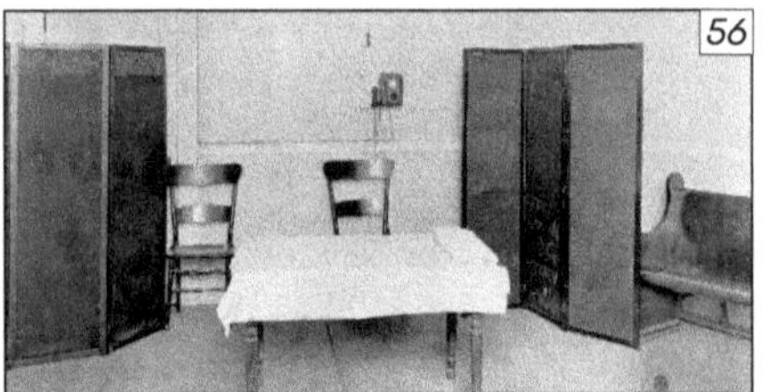

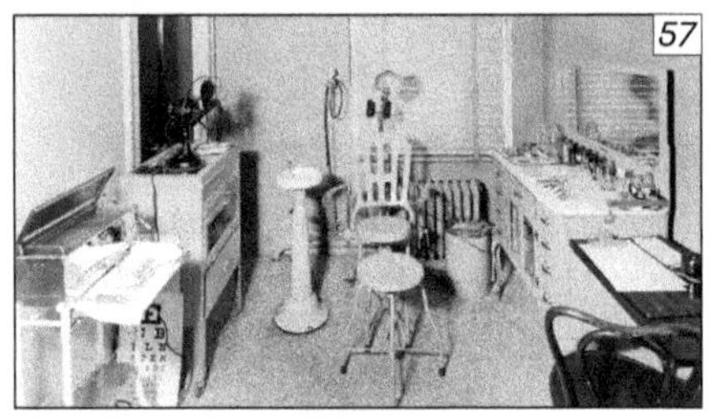

Figure 56: This room in the basement served as the original clinic location inside the First Presbyterian Church. The sign at the entrance welcomed all children. Courtesy of the Dallas Public Library. Figure 57: An examining room in the new clinic was filled with modern equipment that may have looked intimidating to young patients—and their parents. Nevertheless, those sterile metal objects supported the best possible care available to children at the time. Courtesy of Children's Health Archives Center.

All three of these institutions had similar missions: to provide specialized healthcare for children, mostly children whose families could not afford to pay. They shared similar arguments in favor of their missions. Healthcare for children is different than that for adults and requires specialized training for doctors and nurses as well as special facilities. It is a service to society as a whole to improve the health of poor children.

While each was somewhat specialized in what patients they treated, their work often overlapped. The first steps toward future consolidation were implemented in 1941. They recognized that the overlap in their services cost money and efficiency of care. They created an umbrella institution, Children's Medical Center, which also included Hope Cottage, providing care for orphaned babies. While each

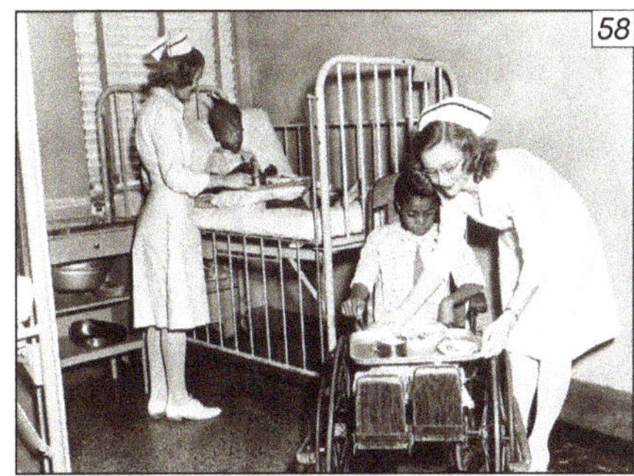

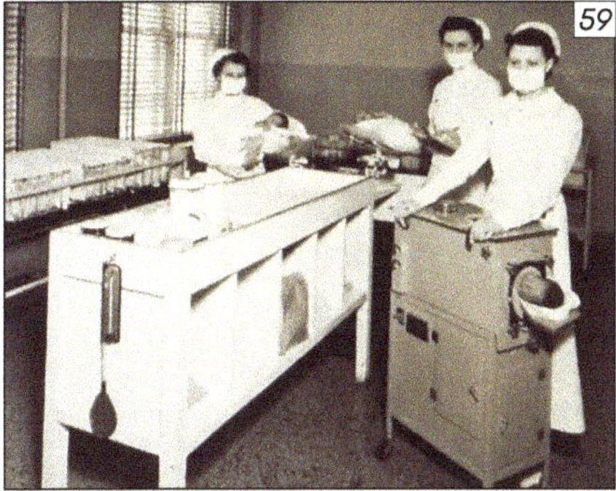

Figure 58: Polio was even more of a scourge for children than adults, and the pace of recovery was slow and uncertain. These children were treated at the new hospital. Courtesy of Children's Health Archives Center. Figure 59: Even as medical science moved toward a vaccination for polio, it raged in Dallas in the 1940s and 1950s, terrifying parents and children. The boxlike machine holding the infant is a pediatric iron lung. Courtesy of Children's Health Archives Center.

remained separate institutions, they divided responsibilities. Freeman clinic assumed most outpatient services. The inpatient care for children over two years of age took place at the Children's Hospital while the babies remained at Bradford. They also began to combine their educational efforts. In the 1950s, those efforts grew to encompass formal teaching of professionals as well as research. This included increased interest in the study of children's behavioral norms and differences.

Research efforts at the Children's Hospital brought national fame and international patients. These efforts included work on pediatric immune deficiencies, and starting in the 1950s, advances in the care of heart disorders and open-heart surgery. Their original goals and large ambitions pushed them beyond the local, social service basis of the other two institutions, positioning them to enjoy the strongest popular association with the growing consortium. Address listings for the Center and the Hospital were the same, 2306 Wellborn Street, by the late 1950s.

The inevitable draw of the growing Southwestern Medical Center relocated the Children's Medical Center in 1967. The address of the new eight-million-dollar facility was 1935 Amelia Street, now Medical District Drive, right behind Parkland. The five-story building contained 200,000 square feet of space. The Freeman Clinic relocated inside the new structure. The third floor housed the Bradford Memorial Hospital.

The city was proud of this shiny new contribution to the Dallas' claim of medical leadership. A local Ford dealership sponsored a newspaper advertisement proudly announcing the accomplishment. Dallas was still in the shadow of the Kennedy assassination and desegregation battles, so any positive contribution to the city's image was welcome.

Apparently having learned the lessons of other hospitals' constant expansion needs, the original structure was engineered to accommodate four more floors. In 1979, three floors were added, as well as a separate building for infrastructure support and a parking garage. The hospital had become the referral center for a variety of types of services. Emergency cases were causing non-emergency treatments to be postponed. Providing referrals allowed non-emergency cases to be addressed quickly at other facilities.

Later expansions into the 2000s were on a vastly larger scale. The Center leased space in the old Menswear Mart on Stemmons Freeway and bought the property in 2005. The former Mart is today the Children's Health Specialty Center, focused on specialized pediatric care and outpatient clinics. The original consortium of children's hospitals had consigned those functions to the modest Freeman Clinic

Figure 60: In 1966, the future site of the Children's Medical Center was a mess of construction materials. Parkland Memorial Hospital is in the background. Courtesy of Children's Health Archives Center.

Figure 61: The completed building. Courtesy of Children's Health Archives Center.

sixty years earlier. Now they needed 400,000 square feet to meet the spatial needs of a growing population and demanding new technology.

The Center has always sponsored medical innovations, expanding their range of care. Prior to consolidation, the Freeman clinic provided modern cardiac care, including the first corrective heart surgery ever performed on an infant, in 1941. In the 1960s, the hospital's new proximity to the Southwestern Medical School insured that patients had easy access to specialists there.

Later innovations for the Center included a pediatric day surgery and Low Birth Weight Clinic. A very successful capital campaign began in 1979. It funded new centers for hemophiliacs and epilepsy patients, as well as increased outpatient heart care, a pulmonary lab, and dialysis. In 1984, Center doctors working with UT Southwestern in the nation's first pediatric-only liver transplant program completed the first such operation in Texas. The collaborating institutions also opened a General Clinical Research Center in 1987 to seek cures for children's diseases.

By 1990, the Center was using a revolutionary ECMO to provide life support by keeping the heart and lungs operational. The following year, they opened the Charles E. and Sarah M. Seay Emergency Referral Center to properly assess the needs of severely injured children. In 1996, they began the yearly publication on the state of children's health and welfare in the county. *Beyond ABC: Growing Up in Dallas County* gathered the relevant statistics to help local governments and community organizations determine how to improve children's lives. In the years following 2000, the Center attracted attention for separating conjoined twins, was recognized as a top treatment center for Sickle Cell, and was the first children's facility in Texas designated as a Level 1 Trauma Center.

In 1988, the Center began a yearly parade in downtown Dallas. The massive effort certainly was different than the early fundraising events for the first children's hospitals. The rummage sales, luncheons, and flower shows were small and mostly carried out by a limited sector of society for the benefit of the less fortunate. They were worthy acts of charity. For three decades, the parade represented giving back to the public while raising funds, and recognized that providing advanced care to all children has become an act of universal love. To bring in 2021, Reunion Tower NYE Foundation conducted a fireworks extravaganza, with Children's Health as the North Texas region's beneficiary non-profit organization.

The small-scale and often grassroots origins of all the institutions of the Medical District might surprise those visiting their massive, modern facilities of the early twenty-first century. Known and unknown individuals built the Medical District. Dr. Edward Cary, Dr. Onesimo Hernández, and May Forster Smith dedicated themselves to medicine. Donors like Karl Hoblitzelle, Thomas Bradford, and Richard Freeman provided the money. Volunteers of all types, whether fundraising to buy cribs for the early hospitals or delivering flowers to patients in the newest Parkland facility, did their part.

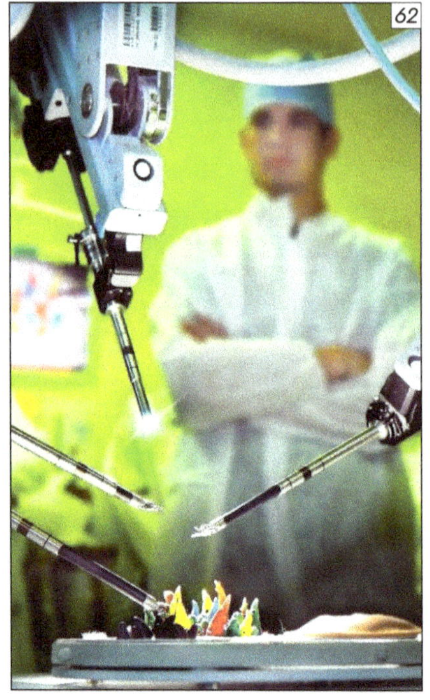

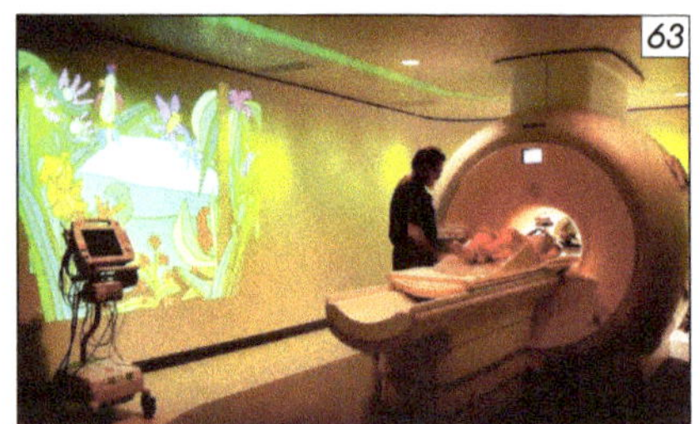

Figure 62: Nobody in the early years of children's medical care could have predicted amazing innovations that would become available—such as robotic surgery. Courtesy of Children's Health Archives Center. Figure 63: Even adults might find modern diagnostic devises frightening, so child-friendly decorations and distractions are used to calm little patients. Courtesy of Children's Health Archives Center.

Natural features and quirks of economics and politics hindered the early development of the land northwest of downtown Dallas. This may have understandably annoyed the residents and landowners there. Transportation limitations in the pioneer days guaranteed that the Medical District attracted hearty pioneers willing to live in semi-isolation. Surely many of those pioneers were quite happy with that situation. Those who craved company could visit Cedar Springs for a bit of community gossip and shopping, but it took a greater travel commitment to reach the offerings of downtown Dallas. Then Dallas itself began to expand, drawing in previously rural residents. It was a long process for the area of the Medical District. Slow and spotty annexation into the city denied the area's few denizens access to city services, and kept away many would-be residents. The result was a landscape of large farm holdings crossed by railroad tracks, within sight of downtown's earliest tall buildings.

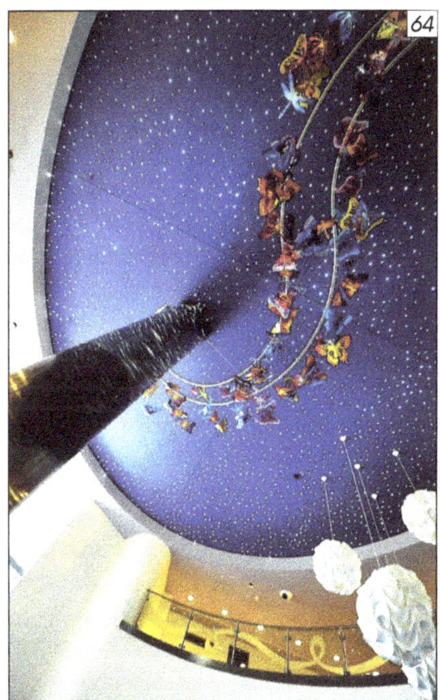

Figure 64: Fun is an important part of healing children, both inside the hospital and out. The butterfly sculptures hanging from a ceiling decorated as a night sky are just some of the bright artworks that entertain patients during their stay. Courtesy of Children's Health Archives Center.

That each step forward in the Medical District was doomed to obsolescence was a good thing: speedy medical progress constantly found better treatments that needed better facilities, equipment, and education for impassioned medical professionals. The largest group of people to experience the growing Medical District over the years has surely been the patients. Arriving with a variety of emotions range from despair to hope, they have experienced the Medical District throughout its growth differently than the people who built it.

The first American pioneers to arrive in the area now occupied by the Southwestern Medical District had big dreams for the land. They could hardly have predicted it would become

Figure 65: Outreach efforts like the parade and fireworks remind the whole city of the work of this important institution in the Medical District. Courtesy of Children's Health Archives Center.

what it is today. They expected the land to support farming and cattle, and it did. They hoped for roads and railroads to connect them to the other places, and those slowly arrived. The idea of an airport would have surprised them! A few may have predicted that their land would eventually change from agricultural uses to urban businesses and homes. Harry Hines Boulevard was unlike any road they could have imagined, but the Dallasites who welcomed its arrival did so with the same sense of hope and pride as those who earlier welcomed the first steam engines.

If those pioneers could read about the new medical facilities that grew in the area, they might remember their excitement at the arrival of Dr. John Cole in Cedar Springs. His informal training and medications concocted by hand were a welcome answer to the people's healthcare needs. He brought healing, as good as could be had at the time. With each decade, the people of Dallas continued to invest in medical progress. As the pioneers well knew, each bit of progress required hard work. The modern Southwestern Medical District exceeds their wildest dreams for the land.

ACKNOWLEDGMENTS

Acknowledging the realization of this book requires a heartfelt recognition of the invaluable contributions made by numerous individuals and organizations. The Texas Trees Foundation (TTF) Board played a pivotal role in supporting and guiding the project, and the dedication of TTF staff, with special gratitude extended to Marinda Griffin, underscores their commitment to the cause. A sincere appreciation is extended to Janette Monear, President & CEO of TTF, whose leadership and vision significantly shaped the narrative. To all those mentioned and the countless others who have played a part, your collective efforts have truly made this endeavor possible.

DR. EVELYN MONTGOMERY
ROBERT PREJEAN, SWMD MANAGER
SUMMERLEE FOUNDATION
SOUTHWESTERN MEDICAL DISTRICT BOARD
DALLAS MEXICAN AMERICAN HISTORICAL LEAGUE
UT SOUTHWESTERN MEDICAL CENTER
CHILDRENS MEDICAL CENTER - DALLAS
PARKLAND HEALTH & HOSPITAL SYSTEM
CITY OF DALLAS
WILLIS WINTERS
JOHN SLATE
ADRE BOWER
BOB IKLE
LANNIE MCCLELEN
ABBY MCGEE
THE DALLAS PUBLIC LIBRARY –
    DALLAS HISTORY & ARCHIVES DIVISION
SOUTHERN METHODIST UNIVERSITY -
    FOSCUE MAP LIBRARY
THE DALLAS MORNING NEWS
JESSICA POWERS, EDITOR & PRODUCTION MANAGER
KATHY MCINNIS, GRAPHIC DESIGNER
INGRAM SPARK, PRINTER & DISTRIBUTOR

AUTHOR'S BIOS

DR. EVELYN MONTGOMERY is an Historian and Director/Curator of the Old Red Museum of Dallas County History and Culture and founder of EvelyninDallas, providing consultation on the topics of History, Museums and Historic Preservation. She was previously the Director of Collections, Exhibits, and Preservation at the Dallas Heritage Village, where she worked for fifteen years and was responsible for 25,000 artifacts. Prior to that, she taught History and Philosophy at UT Dallas and El Centro

Evelyn Montgomery, PhD

College. Evelyn has a Ph.D. in Humanities and History, a Master's in Architecture, and an Undergraduate Degree in Interior Design.

Robert Prejean

ROBERT PREJEAN, Manager and sole employee of the Southwestern Medical District Board, also contributed to the book. Bob obtained a Bachelor of Fine Arts from Southern Methodist University and a Master's Degree in City and Regional Planning from the University of Texas at Arlington. He is the youngest of three children and grew up wandering the banks of Turtle Creek from his Oak Lawn home not far from the Medical District. Collecting information and listening to stories has given Bob an extensive knowledge base of the SW Medical District and region. Time, as the great instructor, will yield a SWMD historical narrative that can solve today's problems by investigating the past development patterns responsible for them while understanding the dynamic ever-changing world of technology and innovation in which we live, a marriage of past and present to expose areas of opportunity and concern.

INDEX